Child Care Marketing Online

The Definitive Guide to Attracting More Families to Your Child Care Center or Preschool

By Devin Murray

"Within 5 days of working with Devin Murray I made a Google search for childcare in my local area and was second in the organic search on the first page. Previously I was on the second page. I continue to be excited about the results. Inquiries, tours and enrollment continue to grow and our program is filling again."-Lynne Sutton, Owner

"Anyone can learn to market with Devin and Kris's fabulous tools, tips, and resources. You can have a full enrollment with a wait list if follow their practical advice!"- Michele Chavez

"My inquiries and tours have gone through the roof. That is a huge success. I very much look forward to continuing this program and putting all that I have learned into play. Thank you so much for all your help and support. I'm so thankful for you!"-Brynn Kelley, Owner

"Not only have we increased the ranking and traffic to our website, and the transition of the number of enrollment inquiries to successful enrollments, but we have noticed an overall increased excitement by our staff in promoting and marketing our program."- Lisa Richardson, Executive Director

The Most Amazing Free Gift Ever

$554.94 of Pure Enrollment Growing Information

Here's the scoop...when you sign up for the Amazing Free Gift package, you will receive:

FREE GIFT #1: Staff Training DVD "How to Put On Your Sales Hat in Early Childhood Without Appearing Sales-Y". A great tool for transforming your staff into your marketing partners. In this DVD, you will get actionable ideas for turning your staff meeting into a strategic session for gaining "buy-in" and partnership from your teachers and directors, in regards to growing your enrollment. This is an invaluable tool for engaging your team and transforming them into your enrollment-building partners. **Retail value: $97.00**

FREE GIFT #2: Audio CD "The #1 Thing You Can Do To Immediately Get More Enrollments for Your Child Care Program". Retail value: $67.00

FREE GIFT #3: Audio CD "The #1 Secret to Becoming a Highly Successful & Profitable Child Care Business Owner". Retail value: $67.00

FREE GIFT #4: Step-by-Step Workbook "Easy Steps for Measuring the Success of Your Marketing & Enrollment-Building Efforts". Most business owners, including child care owners, simply don't keep score of their core business "metrics". This guide will take you through the 9 essential metrics you need to track in your child care program, if you want to easily and quickly grow your enrollment and get to full capacity. **Retail value: $127.00.**

FREE GIFT #5: Special Top-Secret Audio Interview with Ms. X "How I Opened My Brand New Early Childhood Center With a Waiting List of 48 Children". Listen in as I interview "Ms. X" a child care start-up with little to no early education experience. Ms. X opened her new preschool 100% full with a waiting list of 48 children, in an inner-city neighborhood. Use the strategies Ms. X reveals to get fully enrolled quickly, or open up your new location in a highly successful manner. **Retail value: $97.00**

FREE GIFT #6: Two Months FREE TRIAL of Kris Murray's Insiders Circle featuring monthly newsletters, audio CDs with experts each month, actual examples of real marketing pieces, ads, flyers, etc. that you can "model", what's working for other programs around the country, and much more! **Retail value: $99.94.**

www.ChildCare-Marketing.com/AmazingFreeGift

Study with the Author

Looking For More?

Check out the Study with the Author series. Listen as Devin talks you through each chapter and adds additional details answering questions from child care leaders just like you.

- Audio training to accompany each chapter
- Special webinars and audios covering chapter topics pulled from the vault and not available anywhere else
- Tools links and resources to help you achieve more faster
- Much more

Learn more at:
www.ChildCareMarketingOnline.com

Have the Author Speak to Your Group, Association or Company

Devin Murray

Devin Murray is the leading expert in online marketing for child care and early education program. His speeches and training help owners, directors, teachers and staff to effectively marketing online to increase enrollments and family retention. Focusing exclusively on child care Devin understand the unique issues, challenges and rewards. Devin is the author of several books including *Child Care Marketing Online* and *Business Lessons from the Cockpit*.

Devin Murray is available for:

- Conferences (nationwide, regional, state or local)
- Meetings
- Corporate or Association Training
- Web Training and Events
- Leadership gathering
- Seminars
- Keynote Speaker
- Marketing and Sales Retreats

Topics (A brief overview of points covered)

1) **Social Media for Child Care Professionals-** How to utilize social media including Facebook, Pinterest, Twitter and LinkedIn to grow leads, and engage parents.

2) **List Building -** Having a large responsive list is one of the surest ways to guarantee your program is always full. Learn why, and how to grow your list.

3) **Google Places and Maps -** Parents today start their search on the internet. Often this means Google Local Business Listings, Why and how to make sure you are showing up where your prospects are looking for you.

4) **How to Get Testimonials and Review -**This presentation teaches you how to get testimonial and reviews for parents that work. You will learn how and why video testimonials are changing the landscape. You will also learn how to use the testimonials you have on more places than just your website to grow your social proof and enrollments.

5) **Maximize Your Marketing –** Easy systems to save you time and grow your enrollments

6) **4 Pillars of Effective Marketing for Child Care Leaders –** Learn how to create a stable and powerful marketing system that delivers long term success.

7) **How to Get Your Website to the Top of Google -** Having a website nobody finds is useless. In this talk you will learn the easy, step-by-step process to move your website to the top of the search engine

8) **Half Day, Day and Multi-Day Training -** Workshop style training to not only teach how to use technology but to ensure all attendees leave having used and set up their systems correctly.

Why Devin?

Unique selling points...

⇒ Devin is one of only a handful or professional speakers who focuses solely on the child care industry, its needs and issues

⇒ Devin is the author of several books

⇒ Devin is the COO of Child Care Marketing Solutions a company dedicated to educating and help early education professionals

⇒ Devin is a certified Google partner and Google Engage Company Owner

⇒ Devin is a certified educator and instructor with years of experience teaching individuals of all experience levels.

Perfect Audiences...

⇒ Owners who want to worry less about their centers and enjoy their life more

⇒ Directors who want to see their centers full and have more time not less

⇒ Teachers who have been tasked with helping grow enrollment but have never been taught marketing

⇒ Any child care professional who is struggling to understand what marketing is working wants to not waste money of what doesn't

⇒ Anyone who is helping child care owners and directors increase enrollments

---

Did you Know?

- Devin is available for multiple concurrent sessions
- Devin does online workshops so nobody needs to travel
- The same techniques Devin teaches will work to grow your association membership—he can show you how

To check availability contact:

Toll Free : 877-254-4619

Devin@ChildCare-Marketing.com

www.ChildCare-Marketing.com

Warning – Disclaimer

The purpose of this book is to educate and entertain. The author or publisher does not guarantee that anyone following the techniques, suggestions, tips, ideas or strategies will become successful. The author and publisher shall have neither liability nor responsibility to anyone with respect to any loss or damage caused, or alleged to be caused, directly or indirectly by the information contained in this book.

This book is dedicated to my wonderful and amazing wife, Kris, and my two loving and beautiful kids, Owen and Maeve all of whom have stuck by me through the writing of this book and given me loving hugs when needed.

Special Thanks To:

Camille St. Martin for superb editing
without complaint.

Barbara Twachtman and Sidney
Alexander for initial review of this book
and lots of great suggestions to improve it.

TABLE OF CONTENTS

Chapter 1

Who Is This Book For?

As a child care center, preschool, daycare, or early education program you rely on people calling you and coming in for tours. That is the life of your business.

This industry is different from most other businesses in that the clients have a very defined life span as a customer. Regardless of what age they start, you know there is a limit to how long they can stay with you.

They will be forced to leave you when they start school or when they hit the upper end of your after school programs.

This means you know as a guaranteed fact that all of your customers will eventually leave.

This also means you know you need to keep filling the funnel with new prospects and enrollees or you will ultimately go out of business.

If you are in any way connected with helping your program or school grow and stay in business then this book is for you.

So this book is for:

- Owners
- Directors
- Marketing staff members
- Teachers

- Child care centers
- Daycares
- Preschool
- Summer camps
- Before and after school program
- Single school programs
- Multi center child cares
- Franchises

This book is for any business owner who wants to get their business online or improve their existing online marketing.

Why Should You Read This Book?

The landscape is changing and so are your clients. They are becoming more tech savvy and are often much more inclined to do business on the web. The millennial generation, ages 16-35, are now the ones searching for child care. They are using new methods to search for quality providers, such as internet search engines and social media. You need to be found where they are looking.

In the current business landscape, child care centers are fighting tooth and nail for every customer. Unfortunately, most are using outdated marketing methods, IF they are marketing at all.

Let's face it, the phone book is dead. The newest generations of people with young kids are web-first searchers who live on their smartphones and trust the reviews of strangers on Yelp over their neighbors.

If you are not on the web and not easy to find, you might as well not even exist. There are enough other choices out there, and a parent will enroll their child with someone else before they ever find you.

I suspect at some level you already know this, but either you don't know what to do or you don't have the time to act on what you know you should do. If so, this book is for you.

Why Should You Listen To Me?

For the past seven years I have been helping child care programs around the country.

I have always been a bit of a computer nut. I'm one of those people who thinks it is fun to wake up and read the Google blog.

I wasn't always an internet nerd. I started my career path as a professional pilot. I spent almost twenty years flying international jets and even did a stint as a flight test pilot.

But even then I was working with computers. I sold my first computer program to one of the first airlines I worked for.

I also have always enjoyed learning and testing. I like figuring out WHY things are happening, proving them, and sharing my findings with others.

Then in 2005, my second child was born and I wasn't willing to miss all those important days in her life, like I had seen happen to many of my friends.

I landed my plane in Austin, Texas, one day, and simply quit.

I already knew a lot about the internet, computers, and marketing so I quickly began running over 500 websites for a company with an online marketing budget of over $500,000 a year.

Then I opened my big mouth.

By this time my amazing wife, Kris, a marketing expert bar none, had started to help child care centers around the country. As a part of her programs she regularly held live conference calls where owners, directors and teachers could ask questions about child care marketing and how to grow enrollment.

I would often listen in and occasionally lend my expertise about the online world to these calls. One thing led to another and before long I had several clients in the child care industry. I was helping them grow their online presence and coaching them with their online marketing.

This led me to realize the subtle nuances in the business of child care, and the unique issues we all face. So I let all my other clients go and for the last several years have been focused entirely on the child care industry.

I have been helping people just like you grow enrollment, become more profitable, and even reduce the time you spend at work.

I won't waste your time.

I know you are busy, and I respect your time. So the information you will find in this book is easy to read and designed for fast implementation. That way you can get going quickly to create an effective internet presence.

Even if you are not going to be the person actually doing the work, you will find this book helpful. I have designed it so you will gain the knowledge you need to understand what the "techies" are saying. With this new understanding, you will be able to lead your team in the direction they need to go in order to get the results you want.

Chapter 2

WHY THIS BOOK MATTERS

People no longer use the phone book to find the local services and companies they want to do business with. Instead they are now using the internet, on their various devices, to search for these same businesses.

The phone book has now been relegated to an ad hoc high chair or door stop. In fact, in some parts of the country, legislation is being passed to stop the delivery of phone books because they are not being used and going straight to the landfill.

So how are people finding the local companies they want to do business with? Simple – they are "Googling" them. They are going online with their computers, smartphones, or tablets and doing searches.

They are searching and visiting the businesses they find online.

Here is a bit of perspective:

> ➤ 71% of all American adults use the internet. When just looking at the millennial generation, that number is closer to 100%.

> ➤ Over 50% of all purchases are preceded by an internet search. People now do research online as the first step to most buying decisions. The larger the purchase the more research they do.

Only after they narrow down their options do they begin calling and visiting businesses.

This is very true of child care centers. Parents start looking at options online, finding a few near the location they want that have the programs they are looking for. Only then will they call to find out more information or set up a tour.

If your business cannot be found online, these parents will never call you! You might as well not exist to them.

Of all search queries, 30% contain a city, state or zip code. That percentage doesn't account for all the local-based searches. The search engines are smart enough to know when most people are looking for a local business, so some might not even type their location in their query.

If you search "plumber" Google understands you are more than likely looking for a plumber near you, and will therefore return local results. So looking back at that 30%, the number of searches looking for local businesses is probably closer to 50% or more.

According to various online sources, the category of "child care" is the number two local search result, just behind "hotels" in total number of monthly searches.

This trend towards the internet will just continue as the millennial generation grows in power and income. This is the group of people born between 1977 and 1996 who are now 16-35 years of age. This group already accounts for **79% of first births and 68% of all births.**

This is the largest group looking for child care programs, and they are the most connected, online group in history.

Internet searchers are not just looking to find businesses, they are seeking information on the reputation of companies.

A few years ago, we would ask people we knew when looking for recommendations for local businesses or services. We would ask our friends and family, neighbors, or people at churches and organizations. We trusted what they had to say and would use their comments to decide who we would do business with.

Now that has all changed. People go online and use the reviews written by others, sometimes complete strangers, to decide who to investigate further.

You must be putting your best foot forward online.

Realize your ideal prospects are researching you online and making a choice about whether to do business with you long before they pick up the phone or walk in your door.

You need to make sure your online foot print is the best it can be, and shows what a great program you have. Anything less and you are doing yourself a disservice.

More important than anything else, you must be found.

The newest generation of parents has loads of information available to them from a wide array of media sources and will therefore put very little effort into finding you. You need to make it easy for them.

This means you need be where they are looking. And that means being on the first page of Google search results, closer towards the top. Less than half of searchers will scroll to the bottom of the page and less than ten percent will go to the second page.

If you are not at the top of a search results page, your potential client will most likely chose a program that is at the top, even if your program is better.

That is what this entire book is about: Teaching you how to ensure your child care website is near the top of the Google search page and how to completely impress parents online with your child care program.

Chapter 3

UNDERSTANDING THE SEARCH RESULTS PAGE OF GOOGLE

When you go to Google and search for child care in your area, Google returns many different results.

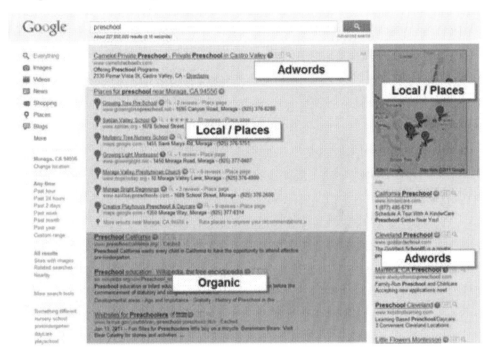

Pay-Per-Click

The Pay-Per-Click (PPC), or Adwords, area of the search results is where paid ads are shown. Google will display either one or

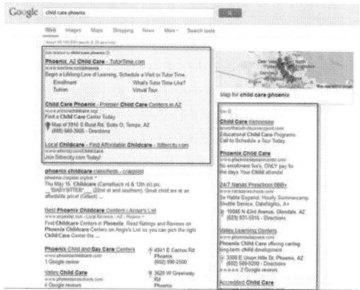

two areas of ads. The top portion will sometimes be left out if Google decides to do so. We will cover these more in the chapter on AdWords.

Natural or Organic Results

Natural or organic results are the search results that take up a lot of the page. These are simply links to web pages. The top results are awarded to the page with the most relevant keywords to the searcher's request. We will cover how to get to the top of the organic search results in the chapter on search engine optimization (SEO).

Local Search or Places Listings

Local Search, or Places Listings, is where local businesses can be found on a map and is usually where searchers look first. Google determines when someone is looking for a local business, and then displays results based on where the searcher is located. This is one of the most powerful tools to help people near you find your program. We will dig in to the secrets of getting on the map in the chapter on Google Places.

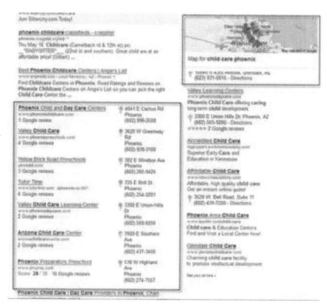

Videos, news, image and shopping results

Depending on what Google thinks a search is about they will also provide these other search results in their video, news, images, and shopping sections. If you have videos, images and press releases about your school there is a good chance they will show up.

Get Your Business On That First Page!

Depending on what options Google provides when a search takes place, you have the chance to have your program seen in several different spots on the first page of the search results.

You could 1) have your PPC ad show at the top, 2) have your organic results at the top of the organic section, 3) have your Google Places listing show up on the map, 4) have images from your program under the images section, 5) have a video you created to educate parents on child care options under the video section, 6) have a news article about how your program is changing the lives of kids in your neighborhood.

If you were a parent looking for a child care center, who would you pick? The program they had vaguely heard about but had to dig to find, or the program that showed up six times on the first page of their search results?

I would bet on the school that shows up six times!

Chapter 4

ORGANIC SEARCH ENGINE OPTIMIZATION

What Is Search Engine Optimization or SEO?

Simply, it is the blend of art and science to get a web page to show at the top of the search results. There is some technical science to it with hard rules, but then there is also a fuzzy art to making it work.

The Purpose of this Chapter

Before we go any further, I want to let you know the purpose of this chapter.

SEO is a huge topic with hundreds of books written on the subject and entire week long conferences where experts do nothing but talk about SEO. I don't think you want that depth of knowledge, nor do you have the need for it. You are already busy enough running your child care program.

If you are a "do-it-yourself-er", I want you to walk away from this chapter with a good understanding of how to do basic SEO. Honestly, unless you are in a very competitive market, the knowledge in this chapter will allow you to be at the top of the results. After reading this, you will know more than 98% of other child care leaders in your area.

If you are a non-technical person who has others handle your online efforts, whether paid or volunteer, this book will give you the knowledge to have intelligent conversations with your team. I want you to be able to ask good questions and understand the answers. You probably have a lot invested in the success of your business, so I want you to be able to lead the efforts online from a place of knowledge.

What Color Is Your Hat?

With SEO there are several different ways to go about getting the end result you want.

"Black hat" is doing work that is against the rules of conduct with the search engines. Basically, it is illegal and, at some point, will get you in trouble. The lure is that it works really well until the search engines figure out what you are doing and how to block it. This is something child care programs want to avoid.

"White hat" is just the opposite and means everything is done by the book with the search engines. The problem with white hat is that it can be hard to get quick results, and if you are up against someone who is doing black hat SEO, it will be frustrating. However, as a child care program, you should really be making sure you are doing everything right.

Gray hat is the in-between; not really doing anything wrong but also not following every rule of the search engines exactly. How far you go is up to you. Just realize where you are and be sure the efforts make sense.

The Algorithm

How exactly does a search work?

All day every day, the search engines are sending out little computer programs all over the web. These programs are affectionately called "bots" or "spiders" because they crawl the web.

They wander around the web looking at every web page they come across. Then they record the words on the page and some other stuff in a big database. They don't actually record the page, just the individual words on that page.

This is all done before a search even begins. All the words on all the web pages are just waiting around to be accessed.

Now when someone is looking for information, they go to a search engine. Google is the biggest, with over 80% of the daily search traffic, but there are many other search engines. Yahoo, Bing and Ask are the next biggest followed by a slew of others.

When someone types in a search, what they are really doing is providing **keywords,** or words related to what they are looking for to the search engines. These keywords can be one (daycare) or many (best child care in Parker, CO).

When someone hits enter, the search engines jump into action. What they do is take the keywords someone is looking for and run it through an algorithm to match it with the database from the spiders.

The goal is to figure out what someone is looking for by their keywords, provide them with the most relevant answers, and do all of this in a fraction of a second.

The search engines keep their algorithms top secret. However, Google does tell us there are over 200 variables in their search algorithm, and on average they make one change per day to that algorithm. They are always trying to improve the quality of the results they provide.

Even without being given the algorithm, we can figure out many of the important variables. SEO experts have been able to backwards engineer the key parts of the algorithm, determining what matters, what doesn't, and what the search engines are looking for to determine which page is in the top spot.

We can break these important factors into two groups – on-page and off-page.

On-page factors are variables the search engines are looking for on your web page. These are things you can directly control, such as the words you use on your page, the places the words are used, and the structure of your site.

Off-page factors are variables you can't directly control. This is how your site interacts with other sites on the web, such as other sites linking to you, referring to you, and demonstrating that you are an authority.

Keywords

Before we go any further, I want you to understand keywords. These are important both on-page and off-page.

Remember the search engines don't really store your page in the database. They only store the words on your page. They don't even store all the words on your page. They drop the a's, the's and other connector words. What is left are the keywords that define your site.

It is only by these words that the search engines can determine what a site is about. Different sites will have different keywords. A dentist and a child care program will use very different keywords. Even a pediatric dentist will use different words from a regular dentist. That is how the search engines are able to return the right results when someone is searching for one or the other.

It is important for you to understand what the keywords are that relate to your program.

Think about them from the side of the searcher. What words would a mother, who just had her first child and doesn't know our industry, use to refer to you?

On-Page Factors

On-page factors are the variables you can control. Regardless of how you edit your site, whether with an HTML editor, like DreamWeaver, or a content management system, like WordPress, you have direct access to update, change and correct any of these.

Page Content
Keywords are how a search engine determines what a page is about. Make sure you are giving the search engines the words they are looking for.

Your home page should have the keywords, generally more than one, that describe your program. You would be amazed at how many times we review a child care website and the home page doesn't contain the word "child care" or "daycare."

If you don't tell a search engine what your site is about with your words, how is it going to figure it out?

As a general rule of thumb, you want your keywords to be used at least once on the page, with a density of between 2-5%.

Here is a great way to check for keywords on any page.

1. Navigate to the page you want to check.
2. Open up your browsers word find feature (Ctrl + f).
3. Type in your keyword.
4. Select "highlight all."

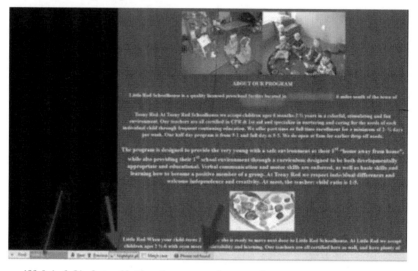

This will highlight all the keywords on the page.

Notice this page, which is a home page, does not contain the word "child care" anywhere on it.

Each page on your site should be about something different so each page should have different keywords. Your home page is about the entire program. Your program pages are about the different programs.

You need to look at each page separately when thinking about on-page keyword usage.

It wouldn't make much sense to have your kindergarten program page with the word daycare used heavily.

Metadata

This is the information you provide to the search engines telling them what your page is about. However, this information is not displayed on the page.

Metadata is still considered on-page because you have control over it and can edit it alongside the page content.

A great way to think of the metadata is to think of each page on your site as a book in a book store.

Title Tag <title>

This is the short title of the page, or what the page is about. If we use the book analogy, this would be the title of the book. It should tell you what the page is about.

The title tag is a very important part of SEO. However, the search engine only records the first 70-80 characters so you need to keep it short.

Obviously this is a very critical part of what your page will be known for. Just like a book, you don't want to read the entire book to figure out its contents. The search engines use the words in the title tag to determine what the page is about.

Because this is so powerful, it is important that you get your keywords into the title tag.

The title tag is also the default wording used when someone bookmarks your page.

You want the title tag to contain the keywords that define your page or program, i.e. child care, daycare, preschool, and your location, i.e. Denver, CO.

To view the title tag on any page, navigate to the page, then right-click your mouse (command click on a Mac), and then select "View Page Source." This will open up a new page showing you the HTML of the page.

Generally one of the first lines will be the title tag shown by the <title>.

The title tag shows up a couple of places on the web.

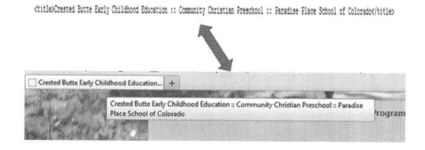

The first is at the top of the user's browser as a file tab. Depending upon the browser setting, only a part of the title tag will be shown. However, if you hover your cursor on the tab the rest of the title will be displayed.

The second place the title tag may show up is in the search results as the bold underlined head of a search result.

\<title\>Crested Butte Early Childhood Education :: Community Christian Preschool :: Paradise Place School of Colorado\</title\>

Crested Butte Early Childhood Education :: Community Chris...
www.paradiseplace.org/
Early Childhood Education is the focus at **Paradise Place** - **Crested Butte's** Community Christian Preschool.

Description Tag <description>

The description tag is a long explanation of what the page is about. This is comparable to the back cover or inside flap of a book.

The search engines will record up to 180 characters of your description, so you still need to keep your description to the point.

You want the description to be two to three complete sentences that flow and make sense.

The description does not show up anywhere on your page visible to people but it can be shown in the search results, underneath the bold underlined header.

<meta name="description" content="Early Childhood Education is the focus at Paradise Place - Crested Butte#039;s Community Christian Preschool." />

Crested Butte Early Childhood Education :: Community Chris...
www.paradiseplace.org/
Early Childhood Education is the focus at **Paradise Place - Crested Butte's** Community Christian Preschool.

Not only should you use the description to tell people (and the search engines) more about the content of the page, but you should also use the space to entice people to click on your listing to view your page for more information.

We have found that including your phone number and address or location in the description helps your

Imagine if you walked into a book store and all the books had the same title and sample back cover description. How easy would it be to find the book you wanted? Not very!

This is what the search engine feels like when you make all the metatags on your site say the same thing. They can't figure out what the pages are about so it penalizes you.

Each page on your site is about something different so give each page a different set of metadata. It doesn't need to be different by much but it should be different.

rankings. This helps tie your web page to your local maps listing.

Keyword Tag <keywords>

The keywords tag is simply a list of words your page is about in no specific order. This tag is used very little by the search engines but can still be useful in helping them understand what your page is about. This can be especially true if your page is about many different items, such as a page describing all of your school's programs.

The words you list in the keywords tag should be on the page or a variant of what is on the page. Listing the variants is a great way to help the search engine display your page in case someone searches for a variant. A great example of this is preschool, which can also be spelled pre-school, and pre school.

There is no maximum number of keywords so as long as it makes sense, add words.

How to Edit Metadata

You can edit metadata right alongside the page content of your site. On a WordPress driven site, you will find the metadata input areas just below the page content area.

Many good themes or SEO plug-ins will tell you how many characters you have used and what the limits are. If your WordPress installation does not have a good SEO setup, All-in-One SEO is a great free plug-in and a generally accepted standard in the industry. You can find it at: http://wordpress.org/plugins/all-in-one-seo-pack.

What To Fix First

When I'm looking to improve the SEO of a child care website, here is the order of effort I find best.

1. Make sure the main pages (Home, About Us, Programs) have good keyword usage in the page content. Make sure each page has the keywords that make sense and in the right amount. If not, make changes.
2. Make sure the home page title tag and description are fully optimized and well written. I can easily spend 20% of my time fixing an entire website just on these two items. Work on them until you get them perfect. Keep rewriting until you can find a way to get everything you want to fit within the character limit. The pipe symbol "|" is a great way to break up segments in the title tag.
3. Make sure the title tags and descriptions on the other main pages are different from each other and in good shape. The key is to tell what the page is about and be different enough from the other pages so as to not be penalized. A great way to make sure this happens is to take the home page metadata and simply add the page name, i.e. Programs or About Us. (Child Care | Daycare | Preschool Hudson Ohio – Programs)
4. Make sure the keywords for all the main pages and the home page are complete and different.
5. Make sure the metadata for all the remaining pages is correct and different for each page. Ensure that the

search engines can tell each page is about something unique. Work on title, description and keywords all at the same time.

6. Finally check the page content of all remaining pages to see that they contain the keywords you think make sense. You will be surprised how many of these pages just don't contain the keywords they should.

The major search engines check and update their records of your web pages daily, if not more often. However, it might take them several days before they start using all of the updates in their search results.

Here is how you can tell when they have fully made the switch.

1. Search for your main keywords or URL.
2. When the search results come up look for the green URL and the "drop down" arrow.

3. Click on the Cached Option
4. This pulls up the current page statistics along with when the page was last cached.

5. At the top in a gray box you will see when the last cache was fully recorded.

This is Google's cache of http://www.childcare-marketing.com/. It is a snapshot of the page as it appeared on Feb 16, 2013 05:36:57 GMT. The current page could have changed in the meantime. Learn more
Tip: To quickly find your search term on this page, press Ctrl+F or ⌘-F (Mac) and use the find bar.

6. When the date falls after when the changes were made and when you see the changes, you know the search engines have completely updated their databases.

Off-Page Factors

The off-page factors are the parts of the algorithm that you cannot control from inside a website editor.

The search engines would like to say you can't control these at all. Although this might be somewhat true, you can influence them.

The off-page factors have some of the greatest influence on the outcome of the search results. The search engines weigh the results this way precisely because you can't easily control what happens off your page.

Remember people trust what others say about you a hundred times more than what you say about yourself.

Links

This is probably the most important factor determining how well you rank in the search results. As Google has told us, they view links to a website as a vote for its quality. The more votes a website gets (links) the greater its value must be.

If no one ever links to a website, then there must not be anything of value on that website. Therefore, there is no reason for a search engine to display that page in the results.

The other side of this is a website that is heavily linked to. This means many people find value at the website, and, therefore, this would be a valuable search result.

All other variables being equal, the website with the most links will be at the top of the search results.

But not all links are created equal. Links coming from a highly trusted website will result in a higher quality vote in the search engines. This is where the entire Page Rank theory comes into play.

Think about it. If CNN was to link to your page, then that should count much more than a page in China nobody has ever viewed.

Again, if all other variables are equal, and site A gets a link from a quality trusted site, and site B gets a link from a low quality site, Site A will show up higher in the search results.

Getting Links

What this means is that it is important to get as many links as you can from the highest quality sites that you can.

How do you do this?

- Get your website listed in all the website directories, especially your local ones. Every state has a list of businesses. Make sure your website is listed.
- Get your website listed in all the child care directories.
- When you partner with other businesses and organizations, ask them to link to you.
- Make sure you link to yourself when making posts on other websites you access, such as Facebook and YouTube.
- Make quality comments on other social media sites and forums with links back to your website. Many times you can do this in your signature.

Anchor Text

There are two basic types of links you can have.

The first is a "naked" link. This is where the website viewer can see the URL. http://www.MurraysChildCare.com

The second type of link is an "anchor text" link. With this link there are words over the top of the link so the website viewer doesn't see the URL. Great Child Care in Denver

What is interesting about anchor text links is the search engines use the anchor text (the overlying text) as an indication of what that website is about. You want to make sure people are using anchor text with the keywords you want to be known for, i.e. Child Care Fargo.

The easiest way to do this is to use a website editor to make the link. Here is an example of that.

1. Type the words to be used as anchor text.
2. Highlight the word.
3. Click the link icon (looks like a chain).
4. Enter the full URL where you want people to go. Make sure you include the "http://," or otherwise it may not work on everyone's computer.

Although search engine optimization is not the most exciting

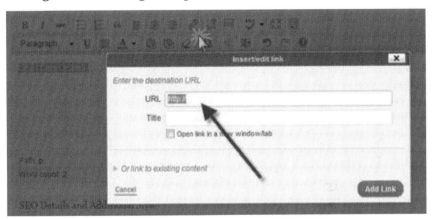

part of online marketing it is still a very important part. It is the foundation for the rest of your efforts, and when you do this well you will find it will help the rest of your online efforts.

Chapter 5

How To Ensure Your Child Care Center Is On the Map

Google Maps and Places are rapidly becoming the go-to place to search for local businesses. In the beginning people mainly looked there for restaurants and stores. Now it has become a habit for people to search for any type of local business by looking at a Maps listing.

This includes child care. In particular the millennial generation has become accustomed to searching the web first. If it is local, that means Maps. Only after they have they done some research on the web, do they call or visit local businesses.

If you want to ensure your child care center is full, you need to be showing up on Google Maps and on the first page of the search results. If you are not there, you will be passed by and never get the opportunity to show why your program is right for them.

Luckily, mastering Google Maps is very easy. This chapter will show you what you need to know, how to get your child care center to the top of the listings, and how to keep it there.

First a Bit of Perspective

Not to overwhelm you, but I want to impress on you how important it is to ensure your program is "on the map." Here are some basic numbers to think about:

- 71% of all American adults use the Internet.

- 91% of all Internet users use a search engine to find information.

- Over 50% of all purchases are preceded by an Internet search.

- 30% of all search queries contain a city, state, or zip code.

- There are 2.6 billion local searches a month.

- There are 5 billion plus cell phone users vs. only 1.8 billion Internet users (almost three times in market size).

- Of these users, 51 million use smartphones.

There is a fundamental shift in how people search for businesses.

The Phone Book is Dead
In fact, some municipalities are going so far as to ban the phone book because all it is doing is being dumped.

People search the web and then call local businesses. The local results page is where people are finding the local services and businesses they plan to use.

How Does Local Search Work?

When someone types in a search that Google thinks is a local term, it:

1. Determines where the searcher is physically located, in one of two ways:

    A. Navigation fix – computer or smartphone fix, if using GPS or other systems.

    B. Computer IP Address or ISP location

2. Looks for businesses that match the search keywords nearby

3. Runs all the nearby businesses that match through a search algorithm to give people the best results

4. Returns both Local/Places search results, Organic (web site) results and Paid Adwords results.

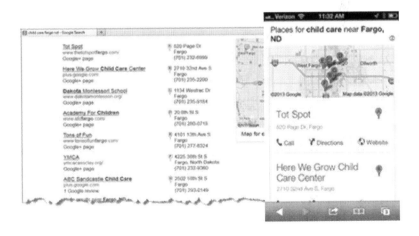

Claiming Your Business Listing

Although there are many different ways to claim and manage Google Places listings, the easiest is to go directly to your Places dashboard and start from there.

Navigate to: http://www.google.com/local/add/businessCenter

Create a separate business account for all your Google efforts. Don't use your personal account. This allows you to give others, such as teachers or contractors, access to the account without them seeing your personal emails in history.

It is best to do it right from the beginning rather than needing to correct it later.

If you have never been to the dashboard before, you will need to sign in with a Google account.

This opens up the dashboard showing you all of the business locations you already have access to.

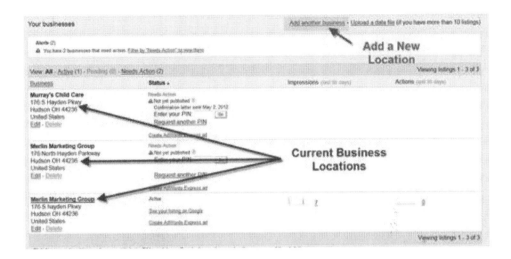

If you have previously claimed a business Places page, you will see it listed here. You will also find the link to add another business on this page. There is no limit to the number of businesses you can claim in one account, but I would consider keeping related businesses in one account. (See side bar on the previous page)

Starting From Scratch
If you have never claimed your business before or it is in another account, you will need to claim it before we can go much further.

However, Google does make it easy.

Click on the "Add another business" link.

Now simply enter the main phone number of your school.

One of two things will now happen:

1. It will find your business page with as much information as Google has already determined or
2. Google will find nothing and will start you with a blank form.

If for any reason you need to change the account you have a business in, just follow the starting from scratch instructions in the new account. You will need to re-verify ownership of the business, but everything will move over to the new account seamlessly.

Either way it is fine. This is just the quickest and simplest way to get the business claimed into the account you want.

Completing Your Business Information

One of the biggest parts of the search algorithm is how complete, accurate and consistent your business listing is. Google's theory is a "real" business will take the time and complete all of the blanks. They also want to see the information in the Google

Places listing to be consistent with other information on the web.

Basic Information

Country: Pick the country where your business is located. For most reading this book this will be the United States, but Google Places is now in most countries.

Company/Organization: This is the name of your business as it would appear in the phone book. I know it is tempting to stuff a location into your name to help with the search, but if that is not truly what you are listed as, this will only hurt you in the long run.

Street Address: This is the address of your school. Be aware Google is looking for consistency across the web, and the address is one of the most common areas where we find issues. This is because the search engines see abbreviations as being different (i.e. East vs. E vs. E. are all seen as different addresses). Pick your address carefully and then stick with it.

Ensure Your Child Care Center is On the Map

City/Town: This is the town where you are located, according to your zip code. I know this can sometimes create issues when the town you are known as and the zip code of the town are different. Generally, we find it best to match what Google is looking for.

State: Pick your state.

Zip: Choose the postal zip code of the area where you are located.

Note: For all of the address section, use the physical address of your school or the main building of your school. Do not use the mailing address or corporate address.

Main Phone: List the main phone number for your school. Again you will want to keep consistency across the web with this phone number so don't use tracking numbers or secondary numbers here.

Additional phone numbers: This is where you can add your fax number, 800 number, and tracking numbers to the list. List as many as you have. This will help with completeness and tying those other numbers to you.

Email Address: This email address does not show up anywhere in your listing. This email is a way for Google to contact you if there is problem or if someone else is trying to change the information on this page. You want this email to be the one you check consistently.

Website: This is the full URL to your website including the HTTP://. If you do not have a website, select the check box, and Google will use your Google Places page as your website.

Description: Google only gives you 200 characters to describe your program. This can be challenging. When I'm setting up a Google Places account for clients, I will spend 80% of my time on this one blank. It is that important. In this blank you want to include two to three complete sentences that describe your program and include the keywords associated with your school.

> "Child Care focused on building strong minds, healthy bodies, and happy kids. Ages 6 weeks - 12 years with focus on reading and having fun. Infant care to preschool, kindergarten and school age programs."

I know that is a lot to ask for in only 200 characters, but you should spend some time getting this just right.

Category: You are given up to five categories to help define your child care. You should use all five. When choosing categories, you can either pick from the list or create "custom" categories.

Always make sure your first category is one of the predefined categories. After that, you can use custom categories.

Warning: Do not put location information in your categories. A category should define a similar business anywhere in the country. Putting locations in is one of the surest ways to get your listing removed from the map.

Country: *	United States
Company/Organization: *	Murray's Child Care Center
Street Address: *	480 BellView Ave
City/Town: *	Crested Butte
State: *	Colorado
ZIP: * [?]	81224
Main phone: *	303-800-6162

Example: (201) 555-0123

Alternate phone:		Mobile phone:	
Fax:		TTY/TDD:	

Email address:	devin@murrayschildcare.com

Example: myname@example.com

Website:	http://www.MurraysChildCare.com

Example: http://www.example.com

☐ I don't have a website.

Description:	healthy bodies, and happy kids. Ages 6 weeks - 12 years with focus on reading and having fun. Infant care to preschool, kindergarten on school age programs

200 characters max, 0 characters left.

Category: *	Day Care Center

Which categories (up to 5) best describe your business?
Ex: Dentist, Wedding Photographer, Thai Restaurant

Category:	Child Care
Category:	Preschool
Category:	Kindergarten
Category:	Infant Care

Note: You have chosen a custom category

Service Areas and Location Settings

As a general rule, select "No, all customers come to the business location." Because in reality, everyone comes to your location even if you go pick them up first. The "Yes" answer is designed more for a business that makes house calls, like a plumber. He is probably coming to you. You are not going to take your leaky faucet to him.

The one exception to this would be if you have a nanny or a babysitting business on the side. Here you might select "Yes" and define the area you serve on a map.

Hours of Operation

Select the "My operating hours are:" option and enter your hours. List the maximum hours you offer even if it is extended hours for an extra fee.

Parents may look at your hours and decide for or against you just from what you have listed here.

Payment options

Pick the types of payments you accept.

Photos

Google allows you to upload up to 10 photos, and you should really consider using all 10. Use pictures that show what is unique about your program and that grab the attention of prospective parents. The pictures should be mini-billboards for your program.

When adding photos, be aware that the first image you add will be used as the main image for your school. In other words, it will be the big image everyone judges your school by. Be sure to put some thought into this and pick an image that shows what makes your program different and unique. Also consider how that image will look when cropped to a square.

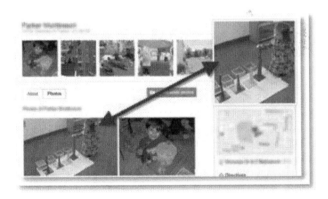

Videos

Google allows you up to five videos and it's beneficial to use all five. You are required to upload the videos to YouTube, which is owned by Google.

Videos are a great opportunity for you to add additional value to your listing. When someone clicks on a video, they will be taken to your YouTube page to view it. From here they can see all of your other videos. Most of these videos should be educational or informative.

Of the five videos you are allowed, here is the best breakdown of what they should be about:

- 30-60 second slideshow showing your center, activities, and kids, or a prepared commercial showing the same materials. This is designed to be an ad for your school.
- Two to three video testimonials from parents. Social proof is amazingly powerful, and video testimonials are some of the best you can have. By showing these videos right on your Google Places listings, prospective parents will be able to view them and use that knowledge to help determine who to call.
- One to two FAQ/SAQ videos. These are individual videos that answer the frequently asked questions or the "should ask" questions parents don't know to ask. These videos give you the opportunity to be seen as the expert provider of information and a resource on the topic.

Additional Details

The Additional Details section is where you can list anything you think is important that has not already been listed. It is done as an item: options list.

This section is a great place to list additional areas served if you service more than just the town your address lists. List schools you service, ages of kids, summer camps, and special programs.

As an option, you can include a URL to a web page. As an example, you can link directly to your summer camp page to allow parents to go there and learn more.

Submitting and Verifying Your Listing

Once you have completed everything and are happy with the listing, you are ready to submit your listing for review and verification. After you hit the submit button, Google will quickly review all of your entries and ensure they meet their guidelines.

You will then be taken to the verification page, where you will be given one or two options.

Google wants to make sure you are the real owner of this business and not trying to claim competitors' listings.

To do this, they send you a verification code you will need to enter into a form. Depending on whether they trust your phone number, you will be offered only the mailing option or the mailing and phone option.

With the mailing option, Google will send you a letter with the verification code inside. It takes up to three weeks, and the

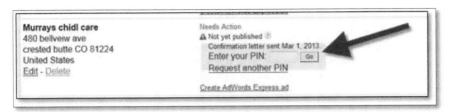

letter does look a bit salesy so keep an eye out for it. I have seen many of these thrown in the trash by teachers and directors by accident. When you get the card, just go back to your Places dashboard and enter the code. You will then have verified the ownership, and your listing will start appearing on the map.

If you opt for the phone method, be at a place you can answer the main telephone number. **Because when you hit call, Google will call you within a couple of seconds**. Make sure you answer the phone quickly and are ready to record the code. Google only gives you a couple of tries to get this right before they will require the postcard verification.

When you get the code entered in the block provided on your dashboard, your new listing will begin to show within a couple of minutes.

Special Note on Changing Your Name

Changing the name of your center can be especially tricky with Google Places, and you should put a lot of thought into how you are going to deal with the name change before you make the change. It all really relates to consistency of information across the web.

Google tracks a business by its name, address and phone number with name and phone number being most important.

Here is the problem:

1. If you keep the old main phone number, Google will see a lot of inconsistency in names across the web and penalize you for this. This means your ranking will go down, or you might even be removed. To fix this, you would need to update all of the listings online with the old name to your new name as quickly as possible. This, of course, assumes you have the ability to update these listings, and they are not controlled by the owner of the old name.

2. If you go to a new main number at the same time you change the name, you avoid the inconsistency issue but are starting from zero in the eyes of Google. This is concerning to them because they don't want to show scam companies to their users. You end up getting put into what is called "the Sandbox." This is where your listing will not show until you earn enough credibility elsewhere on the web.

Overcoming this name change issue can take six months to a year or more depending on how much time and effort you can afford to put into the project. During this time, your new company listing may not show up on Google Maps, drastically cutting the number of inquiries and enrollments you will get.

This is just one more thing you should think about before changing the name of your school. It might be something to start working on several months before the name change takes effect so you have time to build the reputation on the new listing before losing the old one.

Chapter 6

REVIEWS AND TESTIMONIALS

Getting online reviews and testimonials is really rather easy in and of itself. The first and most important step is: ASK.

When parents are happy, they are generally quite willing to make some effort to do a review, but first you need to ask.

When a parent says they are happy with an area of your program, you or your staff needs to say something like "I'm glad you are happy, would you do me a favor and write that down?"

If you are the business owner, you may have to practice this in the beginning. If you have staff, you may need to incentivize them to get reviews. You could offer $1 per review collected, or a bonus for employees if a room gets 10 reviews, like a party or a massage.

Many times that is all it takes; having a simple way for a parent to review you and asking them to do it.

As the internet grows and more people are using it to find local businesses and services, they look at the number and quality of reviews you have. This is why the search engines use the number of reviews as a part of how high you rank in Google Places.

The number and quality of reviews you have also adds to the perceived quality of your business. People first look at the number of reviews and make a decision about your business. Then only after that do they read the reviews to make a choice.

What this means is that if you do not have enough reviews, your child care center may never be given a chance.

The first key to getting reviews is to ask, the second is to make it easy for people, because although they may be happy with your service, they generally will not go through too many steps to give a review.

Ideally, you want people to review you directly online. This makes the process easier and quicker for you. Some ideas to help get reviews online:

- Have a QR code in convenient locations that will take people to your Google Places reviews section. QR codes can be read by smartphones and will take parents online to the page you made to fill out a review. This makes it easy for a parent with a smartphone to complete a review. You could have a sign where

parents check in that says, "Happy with us? Use your smartphone to read this code and write a review." You could also have these QR codes in the rooms and teach the staff to offer this as an option when asking for reviews. Better yet, print it on the back of the hard copy testimonial card shown in the example. (I will go into how to make these QR codes in a later chapter.)

- Have a computer in a good location with desktop bookmarks that will take people to places to review your child care center. If you use a program to log children in and out, you could set this up so a parent can quickly do reviews. If not, you could use an old computer for this task such as an old XP machine stuffed in a corner that can easily handle this task.

- In any online communications that you have with your parents, include links to review sites, and ask them to go there. Online newsletters or emails work great for this.

- Print up a flyer and send it home showing how to give a review.

- All of these can be especially powerful if you are having a special event. Make it a part of the event to give a review. Make it easy and fun while the parent is enjoying your event.

You will not always be able to get people to do a review online. It is a couple of extra steps and too many for some. For those who don't want to go online, make the process easy for them offline.

Have cards like the following example in every room. Print them on card stock so they are sturdy and noticeable, then place a stack by the door of each room, and at the front desk or office.

Now when a parent is happy you or your staff can quickly grab one and get a review.

Now the card here is rather generic. If you wanted you could class it up a bit, but this example will get you started.

Some other ways to get offline reviews:

- Ask for them in your newsletters and parent communications. In addition, celebrate and thank those who do give reviews. People like to be recognized, so by highlighting those who do reviews will encourage others to follow.

- Make it a part of special events. Have a staff member or yourself walking around talking to parents and asking for a review. You might even learn something.

- Mail a card to parents asking for a review. Pick up and drop off can sometimes be crazy for parents, so you may do better reaching out to them in the mail.
- Set a goal to email 5 parents a month, asking for a review or a testimonial. Include the link to the site you want them to post the review to – make it easy for them!

Don't forget about former clients who have left because their child has gotten older, as well as prospective parents. Just because they are not there now is no reason for you to not get a review. Sometimes these can be some of the most powerful reviews you can get.

Video Testimonials
I would be remiss if I didn't talk about video testimonials.

Although these can be harder to put on review sites, video reviews can have a powerful effect. You can place them on your YouTube channel, then either add them to your Places page or allow people to view them.

People like to see testimonial videos; it assures them the reviewer is real.

I suspect in the near future Google and other review sites will either add video reviews or make it easy to link a review to an associated video. Be watching for this and be ready.

Getting video reviews is no different than getting any other review, simply make it easy for the parent and ask them to do it.

To make video testimonials easy here are a couple of things you can do:

- Keep a simple video camera handy. A small Flip for $60 does just fine and most smartphones will record well enough.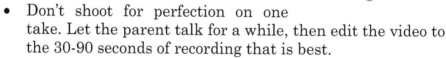
- Have examples. Just like with written testimonials, people like to see what others have done before them. This helps them feel better about what they are doing and lowers the stress level.
- Don't shoot for perfection on one take. Let the parent talk for a while, then edit the video to the 30-90 seconds of recording that is best.
- Don't make them go somewhere to film. This adds effort and resistance to the process. Film them right where they are, whatever the backdrop, not in some back room. I would love to see them filmed right in front of other parents.

Finally have fun with it. If you are doing a great job, which I assume you are, parents will be more than happy to give you reviews. Enjoy the process and it will be even better.

Remember there are two keys to getting reviews and testimonials:

1. ASK

2. MAKE IT SIMPLE

Chapter 7

FACEBOOK FOR CHILD CARE

What is Facebook?

Before we get going with how to set up and use Facebook, I think it would be useful to understand just what Facebook is. This will give you a better foundation about how to get Facebook to work for you.

Facebook is a social network for connecting people with those around them – friends, family, coworkers, or others with similar interests. Facebook started in 2004 as a closed community for college students, requiring users to sign up with a valid university email address.

Today, Facebook is open to anyone over the age of 13. Any person or business can create a page about a particular item or a group about a specific concept. This is where businesses are able to make pages about their company, product or service.

Not only is Facebook is a valuable place for individuals to create a profile and connect with friends and family but it is also a community where brands and customers can interact and create relationships.

Businesses are moving away from traditional marketing efforts, and the customer/business relationship is changing.

The Latest Facebook Statistics

So why is it so important to have your child care business on Facebook? Here are some jaw-dropping stats that will help you to understand.

- 1.01 billion monthly users

- 6.75 average hours per month per user

- 1 out of every 7 minutes online spent on Facebook

- 250 million photos added daily

- 500 million + "likes" per day

- 140 billion friends connected

- On an average day:

  - 15% of Facebook users update their status

  - 22% comment on another's post or status

  - 20% comment on another user's photos

  - 26% "like" another user's content

  - 10% send another user a private message

- Millennials have on average 318 Friends

Personal Profile vs. Business Page

Facebook has two different types of pages you can use - personal profiles and business pages.

Personal Profiles

These are pages set up in Facebook to be used by you as a person. This is designed for you to be social and connected with your friends and others. Depending on your security settings, you must approve a friend request before a person can see your full profile. Before approval there are limited options and information provided to the viewer.

Your profile page is set up and designed to be personal. In fact, you are not allowed to use a personal profile for business purposes. Doing so is a leading cause of having an account terminated.

Business Pages

Business pages, on the other hand, are designed to be used as a business for the purpose of sales, marketing, and communication with customers. These pages give you many additional options and controls that make it safer and easier to work as a business. Business pages also give you a tremendous amount of analytical data so you can better understand how visitors are interacting with your page.

Setting Up a Facebook Business Page

To set up a business page, you must first have a personal profile. This is because Facebook uses your personal profile to administrate a business page. In other words, you control and

oversee businesses from your personal account.

Before you can start the process of setting up a Facebook business page, you will need a personal account. If you don't already have a profile, there are lots of great videos on how to set up a profile. It is about a five minute process.

Don't worry; just because you are the administrator of your child care's business page it is completely separate from your personal page. Nobody will automatically get to see your personal page. In reality you don't need to do anything with your personal page beyond having one.

If you don't have a profile, just get a profile then move on to your business page.

To set up a business page, you have two choices on how to start. If you already have a personal page, you will find the "Create Page" button at the top right. The other way is to navigate to http://www.facebook.com/pages

Either way will take you to the pages page where again you will find in the upper right hand corner the button you want – "Create Page."

Page Category

What type of business are you? Here you get the opportunity to pick from six different types of businesses.

The different business categories allow you to have different options that relate best with that type of company.

As a general rule of thumb for child care programs, choose either "Local Business or Place" or "Company, Organization, or Institution." These work best because they enable you to enter an address and have it show up on the Facebook map tab.

Next, you get to pick the subcategory that best fits your program. Look through the entire list and find the one that most closely matches your business.

Company Name and Address

This is a very important step in the process. One of the biggest issues to keep in mind here is maintaining consistency with your name and address across the web.

You want to use the same name and address here that you plan to use everywhere. If you plan to use abbreviations, such as Ln for Lane, make sure you do that every time with your address.

Finally, you need to agree to Facebook's terms and conditions. Then select "Get Started."

At this point I would skip the profile image. We will return to this soon along with the cover image section.

About Your Company

This section is heavily read by people looking for child care. If you think about it, this would make sense. Choosing a child care center is a very personal decision, and people want to know everything they can about your business. Be sure to include information about your programs and what makes you different from the other programs in the area.

In this same section also include your full website address including the http://.

Next, you will indicate what type of place you are. Child care is one of the best options, but you can type into this box and find what fits best for your program.

Agree that you will be a real company and save information.

The Tour

At this point you will be taken on a tour of your page. If you have not used a Facebook page before, this is a great tour and will teach you about some of the great features and options.

Admin Settings

The admin settings area on Facebook is one of the great parts of a business page. This is where you

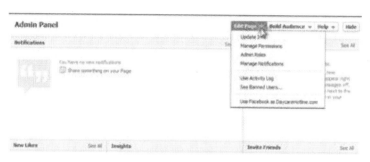

can set who can administrate this page and set up other restrictions. These are safety features, and **you will want to make sure you set them the way you want them.**

Under "Basic Information," you will find areas where you can add a tremendous amount of additional information about your company. To the best of your ability, fill in everything.

Cover Photo and Profile Images

A picture is worth a thousand words, and Facebook gives you some of the best places to put images. The two most important are the cover photo and the profile image.

Cover Photo

The cover photo, or image, is the big image at the top of your page. This is some of the best real estate on the web. When someone first comes to your page, this is the image that will catch their eye first so use it to get the attention of people.

Because this is such a powerful and large image, Facebook has put some very stringent rules on what you cannot do with this image.

These include:

- Can't infringe on anyone else's copyright

- No misleading information or infringing on intellectual property

- Can't encourage people to upload your cover photo to their timelines.

Here are some Do's for your cover image:

- Have a high resolution image

- Have something that contains your logo

- Display your USP (Unique Selling Proposition)

- Make a connection with your fans

- Display social proof

- Make sure to include a description with link

Profile Picture

The profile picture is the second largest image on the page and has none of the restrictions that the cover image does.

The profile picture is a great place to have your logo or a Unique Selling Proposition (USP) photo. Other options to think about are people at your child care, like an image of smiling faces, babies and bright colors.

Both the cover image and the profile image have a huge impact on how people react to your page. That is why it is so important to put a lot of thought into the images you choose before picking them. If you are finding you are not getting good results with your page, you should look at these images to see if you need to update them.

Best Practice for Facebook Business Pages

- Be interactive, fun and helpful.
- Post interesting child care news.
- Be a part of your community. Don't use your page to only sell your program. Make it a place people want to visit, keep up to date on news, and entertain themselves.
- Like other companies and organizations in your geographical area and your industry. This is especially true to businesses you are partnering with.
- Post regularly, when people are most likely to be reading posts on Facebook. As a general rule you want to post daily and in the early afternoon.
- Think visual. Think about posting photos and videos more than anything else. This is what really gets people to read your posts.
- Actively engage your audience. Ask for comments, likes and feedback. Facebook is designed to be social so make sure you are providing people with social content.

Facebook can be a great tool to connect with people that are interested in your business. Make sure you get on there!

Chapter 8

SUCCESSFUL LIST BUILDING

Why Are Lists So Important?

Before we get too far along into how to build a big and successful list for a child care program, we should talk about why having a list of your customers and prospects is so important in the first place.

Simply put, a good list will allow you to make far more money than you could possibly make without a list.

Here are a couple of things to think about:

- 97% of people will leave your website and never return – even if they need what you are offering.

- It takes six or more touches with a business before people will buy.

- People regularly buy from the first business they think of after deciding to buy.

What does this mean to you?

If you have a system to stay in contact and build trust and rapport with prospects and clients, you will be successful.

It is important to remember you need to stay in touch and in contact with your current parents as well. One of the biggest reasons people leave a business or company is because of apathy on the part of the business. The customer feels lost because you have stopped marketing to them, and they basically wander off.

You need to keep marketing to your current parents as well as to new parents.

Irresistible Free Offer

The first step in building a great list is to offer people something in exchange for their contact information. You are asking them to give up a bit of their privacy, and most won't do this out of pure desire to get more email.

They will only do it if they will get something of greater value to them than their contact information. That is the job of an Irresistible Free Offer, or IFO. It's the hook that is so irresistible they just can't live without it.

High Perceived Value

Your IFO needs to have a high perceived value. This doesn't mean it needs to cost you a lot. In fact, it could cost you next to nothing. However, the value to the prospect needs to be extremely high. If you need brain surgery, the best brain surgeon in the world has a very high perceived value to you.

Don't be afraid to create IFOs that talk about your beliefs and philosophy. Although these might turn off some prospects, those prospects would most likely not have made good customers.

However, your philosophies will resonate with the perfect parents for your program.

This will both draw in the right families for you and keep the poor fits from taking up your time.

Point Out the Problem and Solution You Offer

You want to make sure your IFO has to do with child care and helps to point out both the problem you help solve and the solution. You want to be a little self-serving here. When someone finishes consuming the IFO, you want them to understand better the problem they are facing and how best to solve the issue.

Although a free report on how to advance your career in today's economy might have great value to parents, it is not a great fit for you because it doesn't help point out the problem or the solution you offer. However, a free report of how to get homework done without a hassle would be great at showing the problem of getting homework done and hint at the solution of your after school program.

Don't Assume One Offer Will Cover All People

When you are thinking of ideas for your IFO, remember to think what will be irresistible to everyone. You have both left brain and right brain people. Some people will perceive facts and figures as having great value while others will perceive greater value in feelings and emotions.

Also realize people have different ways they like to consume information. Some like to read, others would rather listen to an audio, and still others would like to watch a video. If you match a person's preferred type of media, your offer will have high value to them.

Difficult To Find Information

You want to make sure your IFO is not something a prospect can easily find by searching on Google or by calling your center. If you make one of your offers information on your rates, make sure they can't just call in and be given the rates over the phone.

People are not going to give up their contact information if they can get the answer they want quicker than giving you the contact information.

The Better Your Offer the Better the Quality of the Lead

Your IFO will help you build a better quality list of leads. Higher quality leads will require an offer of great perceived value. Again, it doesn't need to be a high cost offer just high value.

The more thought and effort you put into your IFO the better. A very high quality private pay prospect is not going to give up their contact information for a PDF report swiped from a state agency. Something like that just won't have the value to get them to give up their information. On the other hand, a report about your philosophy on how to get a child to start reading early might have enough value for that person.

Irresistible Free Offer Ideas

FAQ/SAQ – These are some of the most powerful IFOs you can provide because they both raise you to the level of expert in your field and have amazing value to people. These can take a little bit of work to complete but are well worth the effort.

What are they? These are the Frequently Asked Questions when someone inquires about your program. What are the top ten questions you get asked, and what are the absolute best answers you have ever given. You are going to get asked the questions anyway so why not answer them upfront and give a value?

The next set of questions is the Should Ask Questions. These are the questions that parents really should be asking, but because they don't understand the industry as well as you, they don't know to ask these questions. These SAQs allow you to rise to child care guru status in the eyes of parents for two reasons. You are showing them you really know this industry. Nobody else is providing this information so you must be the leader who knows more.

Consumer Awareness Guide – These are very popular words with everyone these days. People do not want to be taken advantage of. They want to be aware of all the information they should know before making a decision.

Top 10 factors to choosing the best child care – People are busy and give high value to anything that will save them time or effort. Lists or checklists are great for this because they consolidate all the information into one quick and simple report. Parents no longer need to figure out what the most important factors are in picking a child care program. You have just provided it to them.

Secret or Insider Information

People always want to know what others don't know. It is human nature to want to be "in" on the secret so provide insider information. It doesn't need to be true secrets just something a non-child care professional wouldn't know.

Activity Guide – Parents are always looking for new things to do with their kids. Providing an activity guide is great for this. Again, you are saving the parents time, and because the kids will enjoy these activities, you must be an expert.

Free Report – The word "FREE" gives a perceived value to anything. These reports are great because you can quickly rotate them for different occasions and continue to provide great value. As an example, you could have a free report on how to deal with time changes and bedtimes right around our change in Daylight Savings Time.

List Management

Now that you have an irresistible free offer to give in exchange for a person's contact information, it is now time to actually set up a system to collect and manage these leads.

To manage your list of contacts and email addresses, you want to use a program specifically designed for the job. In the online world these are called autoresponders.

These are powerful programs that have made it possible to build huge lists that can lead to success as a child care professional.

Control your list

Almost all autoresponder programs make it easy to control your list. They allow you to segment your list into different groups, such as current parents, prospects for infants, and prospects for after school programs.

All the information is stored inside the program so you can access it quickly and search for information without losing it.

You will no longer have spread sheets and pieces of paper with prospects' email addresses on them.

Some of the more advanced programs border on contact management systems in that they will also store a prospect's phone number, email address and a lot of other information you would want.

Comply with CAN-SPAM laws

CAN-SPAM is the set of federal laws governing the use of emails in the United States. Violating any of these rules is technically a federal offense, so as a child care provider you need to make sure you are complying with all the rules. All of the autoresponder programs are designed to ensure you comply with all the CAN-SPAM laws so if you are using one you don't need to worry about it.

You do not want to use your personal or company email system to stay in contact with your list. All it takes is one or two complaints, and you can have your entire email system shut down for violating the CAN-SPAM laws.

Automate your email message

This is probably the best part of these programs. You can set it up once and then leave it alone. You can create an entire set of emails the first time you need them (i.e. prospect, after touring, after enrolling), and from then on, they will automatically be sent out. This will save you a lot of time and energy.

You can send out 1 or 100 or 1000 or

Successful List Building

more emails in a minute. Regardless of how many contacts you have, you can send all of them an email in less than a minute, or you can send emails on a specific day (March 20th) or in a sequence (after 10 days on your list).

By automating the system you can save yourself time and ensure you are always providing the best possible image.

Opt-in Form

The opt-in form is the affectionate name given to the online form used for people to enter their contact information. Modern autoresponders make it very easy to create this form. They all have a step-by-step wizard that walks you through the entire process. When you are done, it either provides you with the HTML code or allows you to email it to your webmaster.

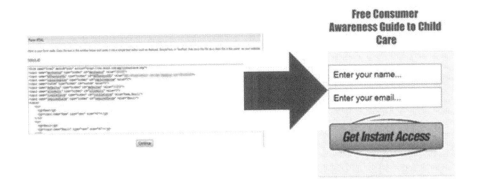

Where do you put this form?

1. **Static page on your website** – and ideally on every page of your site. From the search engines people can land on your site at just about any page. Put your form everywhere.

2. **Squeeze Page or Site** – These are sites or pages on your site designed to help you get a person's information. They are designed without a navigation bar and the only option a person has is to either provide you their contact information or leave. The draw is your IFO, and it will get people to take action. Squeeze pages are best used when you are paying for traffic to your site, such as with Google Adwords or a newspaper ad.

3. **Light Box** – These are boxes that appear at a specific time and gray out the background of a website. They can be set to activate after a specific time or when someone tries to leave a page. They can also be set to only appear to first time visitors.

These are a great way to add an opt-in form without the need to redesign your website.

4. **Float In** – Like the light box, a float in only appears after a period of time. What makes these great is that they simply float in from a side of the screen. The user can still read the page and navigate around if they want. We have found the action of floating in draws attention to the form.

For example, the "Wait...Before You Go..." bar at the bottom is not there when you first come to this site but floats or rises up into view after about 20 seconds on this page.

5. **Offline** – Yes, you can use these opt-in forms to grab the contact information of people you are marketing to offline. Basically, you drive someone to get your IFO at a website that contains your opt-in form, such as with a post card, newspaper ad or even your phone book listing.

Email marketing and autoresponder companies

- Child Care CRM
- Constant Contact
- Aweber
- Mail Chimp
- Many more

Find the system that works for you and has the ability to grow. It is best to take a look at each one. Many of these have free trials so you can explore and see how you like the program and user interface.

Spend 30 minutes with each one and experiment. See if you, or whoever is going to run your list building program, can figure out the program and get it to work.

Building the RELATIONSHIP

Building a list is only the first part of a successful list building program. The second, and most important step, is to have a system or plan to convert your list into paying enrolled customers.

The key here is to have that plan! Remember with an autoresponder system, you only need to create this once, and it will always work for you.

Have an idea of what you want the end result to be from your list building efforts. Are you looking to increase current enrollments, are you looking to grow your social media following, or are you trying to build a list of prospects for a program you have not even launched yet? Know what outcome you are looking for.

To build this relationship, you want to create a sequence of emails to be sent out that help build rapport with prospects and that tell your Unique Selling Proposition, or USP, to illustrate what make your program different and unique.

People do business with other people they know, like and trust. By building rapport through email, you will increase the chances that they like and trust you because you are letting them get to know you.

One of the easiest ways start this relationship building is by weaving the story of what makes your child care program stand apart from everyone else. People love stories and love to learn about why you are different and better.

When you are creating this sequence of emails, you want to make sure it contains quality content and a marketing message at the same time. You want to make sure you are including both. I know it is very easy to include great content yet hard to put that marketing message in there.

Remember the point of your list building efforts is to grow your enrollment. If you are not including some marketing messages, people will not know what to do, and your efforts will be wasted.

When creating these emails you also want to mix in both informative content and entertaining content. Parents will simply not keep reading your emails if all they contain is educational content. Even if they need it, people will become bored and move on.

That is why you want to make sure you have a fair amount of entertaining content in your emails. Stories are some of the best entertainment features you can include. Also include information about yourself. People do business with people, and your program must have a personal face for people to get to know, like and trust.

You want to be open and provide general information about yourself and your program but not too much information. Those of you who know us and have read our emails know our son has ADHD and that I was seriously hurt at work several years ago. This helps people to bond with us and realize we are real people. Feel free to open up and let parents know something about you as a person.

Get the Emails Opened

You can have the best email content in the world, but if people don't open your emails, they will never get read.

The thing that gets people to open their emails is the subject line, plain and simple. This is what catches people's attention and tells them what's in it for them.

First, you must catch their attention. You are competing against the dozen or more emails in their inbox. If your email doesn't stand out and grab their attention, it will either get deleted, or more likely "saved for later," and never read.

People will want to know what they will get by reading your email. Their time is valuable, and they don't want to give it up unless they get something great in return.

Use your subject line to grab people's attention letting them know what is in it for them.

Here are some great examples:

- "Finding The Best Child Care Facility For Your Little One Does Matter"

- "Who's Smarter: Kids or Dogs?"

- "5 Surprisingly Easy Ways To Make Kids Smarter"

To keep getting your emails opened, you need to provide prospects with valuable relationship building content.

If somebody finds your first couple of emails interesting, they will keep opening them until you give them a reason to stop. This is where the entertainment and stories can really help.

Make sure your emails are not just about sales. People will see through this very quickly and quit opening your emails. People do not want to be sold, but they do want to have a relationship with you so weave your sales message into your emails as a part of the entertainment you are providing.

First 1-2 months of your emails should be scripted

These first couple of months are the most important to building the relationship with your list. After the first month or so, people will forgive you for a small blunder but not at the beginning.

You will need to put some thought into sculpting the first couple months' worth of emails. With these you want to:

- Point out the problem you solve. Don't leave it to chance people will truly understand that problem. Point it out.

- Build a relationship. Give people the chance to get to know, like and trust you.

- Overcome objections. Use these first couple of months' emails to overcome all the common objections people might have for choosing your program.

- Be seen as the expert. This is where the educational parts of your email become important. By becoming the go-to expert in your area, you will elevate both yourself and your program.

After the First Couple of Months

After the first couple of months are over, you will have built a strong relationship with your list. They have become accustomed to opening and reading your emails and have learned something about you.

At this point you can relax a bit and only need to worry about scripting your emails for key sales times or as you feel the need for special occasions.

No matter what, you should email people at least every other week. If you wait any longer between emails, you might be forgotten.

Seventy-Two Touches?

One of our clients recently told us they finally secured an enrollment with a family they "touched" 72 times with marketing messages and follow-up campaigns — mostly via email. This family initially chose a different preschool than our clients, but after nearly a year of relationship-building, the parents switched schools and brought their child to enroll with our client.

This happens more often than you might realize! Don't make this mistake. Build your list and communicate to them often and effectively.

Chapter 9

ADWORDS AND PAY-PER-CLICK FOR CHILD CARE

How Adwords Works

When it all comes down to it, Adwords is really very simple. It works this way:

1. You bid on keywords you want your ads to show for. Keywords are the words you think people will be typing to find your services, i.e. "child care."
2. Google picks the winning bid based on many criteria, not just price. Google then picks the second, third, fourth, and so on, up to ten.
3. Google displays the ad for people.
4. When someone clicks on your ad because they find it interesting, you get charged but not before that. You only pay when someone clicks on your ad, hence, pay-per-click (PPC) advertising.
5. Once someone clicks on your ad, they are directed to any web page you desire. This could be your website, a special website, or anything. In fact, you could send someone to your Facebook page if you want.
6. You can then set up Google to record who takes the actions you want them to take after the ad, like filling out a form to request a tour.

Why Google Adwords is Great for Marketing

Google's Adwords gives you, as a child care provider, many great opportunities and advantages in advertising. These include speed, testing, reach, and the ability to track your marketing return on investment (ROI).

Speed

One of the great things about Adwords is the speed it offers you in marketing.

With traditional marketing or even online search engine optimization, it can take months from the time you decide to start marketing to the first inquiries you will receive.

Just think about how long it takes to even run a newspaper ad if a parent tells you they will be leaving. First, you need to write the ad and get it to the newspaper before the cutoff date. Even with this, the ad might not run until the following week. It could easily be 10 days before you start getting leads to fill that vacancy.

On the other hand, with AdWords you can start marketing and getting leads with minutes of the parents' notice. All you need to do is walk into your office, sit down at your computer, and switch the predesigned campaign from "Pause" to "Active." Within seconds Google will start displaying your ads and getting you traffic.

Testing

Adwords gives you an amazing ability to test marketing and find what is working with very little time, effort, or money.

Google will tell you what ads people are clicking on and what search terms are causing your ads to show. This means you will know, not guess, what is getting people's attention.

You can find what offers are working for different groups and take those proven offers to flyers, postcards, and other ads.

Adwords is also a great place to test new programs and offers. For just a couple of dollars, you can see if people in your area are interested in a new program.

Reach

With Adwords, Google allows you to select the targets for your ads. This gives you the ability to reach prospects you would not be able to reach otherwise.

You can target neighborhoods, cities, and even other states you could not reach with maps or organic website results.

You can target keywords that would take far too long for you to get good results within a website. Programs, like summer camps, that you only run for a short time every year would take months of your time to get to the top of the search pages. However, with Adwords you can be at the very top and marketing whenever you are ready.

Here is a secret with Adwords. Because you are targeting keywords, or the search terms people type into Google, you can have your ad run when someone types in your competitor's name. This big secret allows you to reach people who are only looking at your competitors.

Track Return on Investment

Because you are able to track exactly what Adwords is costing and what the end results are (like enrollments) you can accurately track your return on investment.

This is extremely hard to do with many other forms of advertising. Many times you are relying on your prospects to remember and accurately tell you where they saw your ads.

This ability to track and measure allows you to optimize your other marketing with the results you find in Adwords. With Adwords you can find what offers are getting people to sign up and then send out a postcard mailer you know will work.

5 Minutes to Your First Ad

1. Set up your Adwords account at http://www.google.com/adwords/.
2. Select "Create your first campaign."

3. On the next page, you will want to name your campaign. Pick a name that makes sense and gives you a good idea what the campaign will be about. Over time you will set up multiple campaigns for different reasons. Don't worry too much about this. You can always change the name.

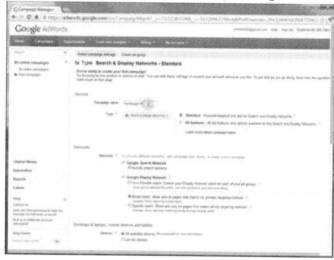

4. Pick the type of networks you want your ad to display on. My general rule when starting out is to use "Search Networks Only". This will help reduce your costs while you get comfortable with the

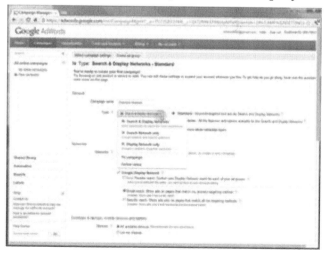

Adwords and Pay-Per-Click for Child Care

Adwords system.

- Search Network Only – This means your ad will show up on Google search results and their major partners. With this selected, your ad will only be shown on pages containing search results for people who are looking for your services.
- Display Network – This means your ads will appear on content websites through the Google AdSense program. With this your ad will only appear on a website that displays Adsense and will be either inline with or on the sides of normal content. People on these sites may not be looking for your services and are generally not shopping.
- Search & Display Networks – This combines both types of networks and will show your ads in the largest amount of places.

5. Now you can pick the location where your ad will be displayed. Because we are really only interested in people that are searching from somewhere nearby, we will want to pick the "Let me choose…" option. This will allow us to pick the town or area our school is in. Enter a zip

code or town name and select from the provided options. Most of the time, I find Google has done a good job of providing the right sized area.

6. Finally, set a budget that you are comfortable with. This is the maximum amount Google will charge you per day. If your ad does not get enough clicks during the day to use all of your budget, Google will charge you less. If your ad gets too many clicks during a day and all of your budget is used, Google  will stop displaying your ads for the day. Be sure to set a budget you are comfortable with, especially in the beginning.

7. Select the "Save and Continue" button to move to the next page where we will write your first Adwords ad.

8. Select an Ad group name. Ad groups are a subset of campaigns and allow you to group similar keywords and ads together. Choose a name that makes sense to you and will allow you to understand the ads and keywords that it contains.

9. Write your first ad.
   - The headline is designed to grab the attention searchers. You want to make sure your keywords are included in the headline. So, if this is a Daycare Ad group, you would want keywords to

include daycare, daycares, and day care and have the headline contain the word daycare.

- Description line 1- Here is where you want to tell people the benefit of clicking your ad of your

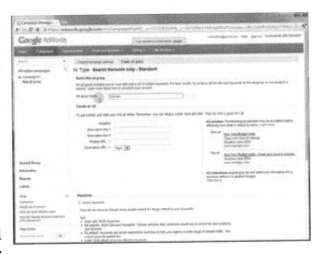

program. Don't make them guess at what they will gain. Come right out and tell them.

- Description line 2 – On this line continue with the benefit from line 1 if you need to, but the real point of this line is to give people a call to action (CTA). Tell them what to do, call now, click

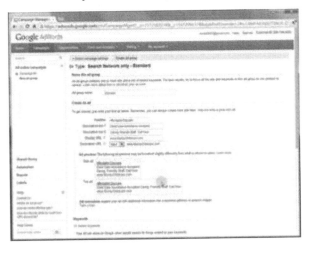

here to get your free report, or learn more. Remember people will be reading these quickly so really let them know what you want them to do.

- Display URL – This is the URL, or website address, that is displayed in your ad. It does not need to be the exact URL you are sending people to. It only needs to be from the same domain. This allows you to integrate your call to action and benefit into the URL and test results. As an example, I could be sending people to a page where they can get a free report on finding the right child care for their needs in our town. That page might be www.murrayschildcare.com/child-care-report-in-hudson. However, I could have the display URL be MurraysChildCare.com/Free-Report. Which one is more interesting to you?

- Destination URL – This is the actual URL where you are sending people. People never see this URL in the ad so it can be long and ugly if you want. You can send people to any page on the World Wide Web, but it is best to send them to a page that talks about your keywords and allows you to capture their contact information. The Ad preview section will show you what your ad will look like both if it displays at the top of the page and if it displays along the side. Rework the ad copy until it reads well and looks like you want it to look.

10. Select the keywords that will trigger the display of this ad when someone searches those keywords. These are going to be the words someone local would be searching for because we set the area of the campaign to be our local town. This means people will be searching for both generic and exact terms, plus variations, so make a rather large list  (daycare, day care, daycare Hudson, daycare Hudson Ohio, quality daycare).

11. Set up billing. Google gives you two basic options for billing, but either way you need to attach a method for payment, generally a credit card, to the account.

- The first form of billing will allow Google to charge your credit card daily for the budget you have set or the amount billed, whatever is less. This is simple and removes your need to add money regularly. However, if you are not paying attention and the budget is set high, you can burn through a bunch of money.

- The second option is to add money from your credit card to your account. Google withdrawals from the balance as your ads get clicks. This is great because you can deposit what you feel comfortable with spending and you will never go over this. The downside is you will need to regularly add money to your account, which is just one more thing to do.

- What is the best way? This is no right answer. Pick the option that works best for you.

12. Your first ad is ready to run and will be displayed in a couple of minutes. Congratulations!

Once you get your first ad up and running, you will probably want to repeat the process and create a new ad group for several other sets of keywords.

The next ad group might be for child care, and you would include keywords related to child care, include the word child care in your headline, and have the destination URL be more about child care.

Testing

You will quickly get comfortable with Adwords, and once you do this, you will want to start testing to try and find what works best for your group of prospects. I always believe in testing at least one thing all the time.

To start a test, simply create a second ad inside an ad group. Google will show the ads in such a way that the ad with the greatest results will show more. After a while you will begin to see which ad is doing the best, delete the other ad, and start a new test.

What should you be testing? Here are some of the first things I test:

- Headline – Change up your headline to see if you can come up with a more attention getting headline.
- Benefit – Change up the benefit to see what resonates with people. This is a great place to use Adwords to see what people are really looking for.
- Destination URL copy – Send people to different pages and see which page gets people to take the action you want.

Pretty soon you'll be able to maximize the money you are spending on Adwords and understand what works for your business.

Chapter 10

UNDERSTANDING MOBILE

Mobile internet usage is being driven by the popularity of smartphones and tablets. These devices allow people to access the internet from just about anywhere.

This ability to check emails, access social media, and do research from anywhere have become a powerful and liberating tool for users. People are no longer stuck waiting to get back to the office or home before they can research the answers to their questions.

Although mobile is great there are a couple of downsides that you really need to understand to help your child care center get the most out of mobile platforms.

Speed

Even the latest high speed mobile internet systems are relatively slow at passing data. It is challenging to transmit data through the air. As an example, 4G networks deliver up to 5 megabits of data per second, as compared to my land line internet connection at almost 15 megabits per second. That is a huge difference when you think about how long a webpage will take to load.

Big flashy pages with videos and graphics might work on laptops and home computers but can be painfully slow on mobile devices.

Add to this that mobile users are on the go and a lot less accepting of slowness. They are walking, driving, or out with friends and if your page doesn't load right now they will just hit the back button and move on.

Operating System

Mobile devices have a special operating system language that is different from a home computer. A mobile device has a lot less memory and uses a lot less energy than a typical computer so this means it has to have a special operating system.

One of the biggest ways mobile device makers has found to save memory and battery life is to simply not program them to handle some internet features. The biggest of these is Flash. You will find a lot of mobile phones and tablets (including all Apple devices) don't display or work with Flash players.

This means if your website is a flash-driven site it will look great on a desktop and be completely blank on an iPhone or iPad.

Screen Size

Screen size is by far the biggest issue you must deal with when looking at mobile devices. My desktop computer screen is 15 inches across, my iPhone is 2 inches. That is a lot less space to display information.

If you try and use the same website that you use for a desktop on a mobile phone you will find the screen so small it is unreadable or that a person needs to scroll all over the place just to read it.

Understanding Mobile Surfing Habits

Before we get into how to deal with these issues on mobile devices it's a good idea to understand how a lot of people end up on your site, viewing it on a small screen.

The two biggest ways we see people get to websites on mobile devices are from emails and social media.

Modern, on-the-go people read their email on smartphones and tablets. 41% of all emails are opened on mobile devices and that number will just continue to climb over time. Even when people are at work they will read personal emails on their smartphone.

What this means is that if you put a link in an email, say to sign up for a parent's night out, the odds are high they will read that email on their iPhone and click the link taking them to your website.

If your website is not mobile ready they will be confronted with a compressed screen that is hard to read and most likely won't be able to enter contact information. The easiest thing for them to do is hit the back button and "get to this later". However this usually won't happen because that email will be buried and forgotten about within thirty minutes.

The other big way people get to your site from a mobile device is through social media like Facebook. Now more than half (57%) of people access Facebook from a mobile device. People socialize on social media and this is often done on the go.

This means if you or someone else puts a link in a social media post there is a great chance people will click that link on a mobile device.

Social media can even lead to people coming to your site without a link. If someone finds your child care interesting on social media they will often simply research you right then and there. They will even go so far as to decide whether they want to enroll with you or not while sitting at a restaurant eating lunch with friends.

It comes down to this... if people can't find what they need to make the decision to do business with you while on a mobile device, they will take the easy path and rule you out.

Mobilize Your Website

I hope by now you see the value and need to have a website that looks good and is functional on mobile devices.

But what does a mobile site really need to have?

Needs to be simple

People on mobile devices don't want a completed website with all kinds of information and details. They want the bare minimum facts. They know if they are interested enough they can always return to your site to get more details.

So if, for example, you are doing a parent's night out promotion, a mobile site would have the sign up information and basic details (time, location, cost, how to sign up) at the top and in large print. That might be all that you need because people generally have come to this page because they were sold on the idea somewhere else and just need to sign up.

Needs to have simple navigation

Mobile users will not browse through twenty pages of content looking for information the way a desktop user will. They don't want to spend the time, so your navigation needs to be very basic and only directed to the main pages. Drop down menus are impossible to use on mobile devices so stay away from them.

Just let people get to the most commonly needed pages - Home, Programs, Location and Contact Us. If you have a blog that could be a good mobile link too, so they can read your posts, but other than that too many choices will probably confuse people.

Needs to be fast loading

Remember a lot of mobile users are at internet speeds similar to dial up – SLOW. So although pictures might look great on a desktop you should limit them on mobile sites. And the ones you do have should be sized very small since people are looking at them on a 2 inch screen.

Videos should also be considered. These can make a website very slow to load. Unless you are using a mobile compatible video player like YouTube I would suggest staying away from videos on mobile sites.

Speaking of things to stay away from on mobile sites, for now skip Flash players. Knowing that videos, graphics and animation done in Flash will not be displayed on over half the mobile devices in the US means you should try to avoid this.

How to Get a Mobile Site

The quickest and easiest way is if your site is built on Word Press. You can add a plug in that will make it very easy to create a mobile website. One of my favorites allows me to build a mobile version of webpages that detects and uses the mobile page for small screen mobile devices.

There are some other great Word Press plug-ins that just take your current content and resize it for mobile devices, such as Mobile LPS, and Wordpress Mobile Pack. This way you don't need to redesign or do any work on your website.

Another option for enabling a website for mobile is to have it designed in such a way that it will automatically resize itself to the size screen someone is using. A lot of these programs will also change the navigation when the screen gets below a certain size. This is a good option is you are not on Word Press and looking to do a completely new website.

A third option is to have a completely different website for mobile users. Often, it will be put at a mobile subdomain, i.e. mobile.amazon.com or m.facebook.com. These standalone sites have advantages that are not constrained by the regular site and can have a completely different structure. The problem is you have to maintain two websites.

When us'ng a different website, your main website senses a mobile device and it automatically sends the visitor to the mobile site. This happens seamlessly.

To get the most out of your website you need to have a site that looks good on a mobile device. The number of smartphone users continues to grow daily and you can be sure many of them are looking for local child care.

Chapter 11

QR Codes "101"

What is a QR Code?

QR stands for Quick Response and at the risk of getting technical it is a graphic representation of a binary message.

Computers talk in a language of 1s and 0s. And when you look at a QR code you will see this language. There are some squares that are on and some that are off. This means a QR code can be any message you want it to be. It can be a URL to a website, instructions to download a file or even the information on a business card and computer directions to create a new contact. Really, anything.

One thing to remember is that the more complex or long the message the larger and more complex the image needs to be. Take these two QR codes. They are both going to the same website but the top one contains a lot of tracking information while the bottom one is a much simpler URL.

So what are QR codes and what do they do?

QR codes are a great way for you to take people who are offline and take them online. Most smartphones with a camera have the ability to scan the QR code and learn more about your program or offer.

This means you can take someone who is reading a paper or brochure with a QR code directly online to your website or to your consumer awareness guide.

It is also interesting how a QR codes plays on our curiosity. People want to know what is behind the door, where the QR code will take them. How many of you scanned the codes on the prior page to see where they took you?

How to Make a QR Code

1. Determine the location URL. You want to send the person to a page that will give them what they are expecting. If you said "Scan here to get our free Consumer Awareness Guide to Child Care in Ohio" then that's the page the person should either be able to access or enter opt in information to have the report emailed to them. Also realize they are most likely on a mobile device so you want to make sure you are sending them to a mobile enabled webpage.

2. Set up tracking if needed. You want to be able to measure the results you are getting so you need to have some type of tracking. It could be that this QR code is the only way to access the web page or special offer. Or you might need to use Google Analytics URL builder (https://support.google.com/analytics/answer/1033867) to enable your website analytics to track the results.

3. Shorten if needed – The longer the URL the more complex and larger the QR code will need to be. I like using Google's URL shortener (http://goo.gl/) or Tiny URL to take complex and long URLs and turn them into small URLs.
(I.E.http://enrollmentbootcamp.com/member/?utm_source =bonus-webinar&utm_medium=web&utm_term=bonus&utm_ca mpaign=webinar-qr becomes goo.gl/J3HSC) This is especially important if you will be printing the QR code small.

4. Create and download the code. I use www.BeQRious.com which has a free service to allow you to create high quality QR codes and a paid service which has some additional features and tracking options. The process is very simple. Just enter the URL and the program will create the QR code.

5. Test. This is a very important part of the process. Make sure the QR code does what you expect it to and is at the size and quality you expect. I've seen on too many occasions child cares test the QR code on their office printer then reduce the size and send it to outside printers. What came back from the printers the code was not readable by a QR reader so all their time and effort was wasted.

How and Where to Use QR Codes

So now that you know how to create a QR code what should you do with them?

- REVEAL something: a story, a video, a "secret"

- ASK them to give back / donate

- Get people to enter a contest

- Get people to follow you or connect with you online.

- **ASK for feedback / reviews**

Using a QR code is a great way to get testimonials and reviews online. When you do a great job parents are more than happy to give you a review. The biggest  issue is the time and effort for them to do so. By having a sign like this at the check-in/check-out station or on cards in each class room whenever a parent wants they can quickly and easily leave you a review.

QR codes are not a fad and will be with us for a long time. Have fun with them and use them anytime you are doing marketing offline.

Chapter 12

FINAL THOUGHTS AND ACTION PLAN

To fill your child care program and to keep your school full you need to be where the parents are, and this is on the internet.

Even if you are not a big fan of the internet and not a "computer person" you need to realize young people who have kids and are looking for a child care program are constantly on the internet. That is where they are looking, first and foremost, for the businesses they want to work with.

If you don't have a website that is easily found there is a really good chance your ideal prospects don't know you exist.

As you get into using the materials in this book you will find the internet is really a fun and exciting place. You can reach and connect with potential clients, friends, and families like never before and at a cost that can't be beat.

Take small steps and push your comfort zone a bit. Don't let this process overwhelm you. Just like a baby learning to walk it will all come together very quickly for you.

You – Personally – Don't Need To Do All This

Your time is worth a lot and if you are like many of the other child care leaders I've work with there is always more on your plate than can possibly get done. Invest your time in the areas where it will get you the greatest returns, and that is in managing the process.

Ask around and check with your teachers, I'll bet you have at least one who would love to tackle your online marketing. The younger teachers are already living online, they are probably of the millennial generation, so let them do the work but understand what needs to be done and lead the team.

Not only are they more comfortable with online work, they will probably be able to get the work done much faster than you could.

The Online World is Always Changing

The online world is an ever changing and updating world. Sometimes it is great, sometimes it is frustrating.

Most of the time, the changes are made to enhance the experience of the user. That is a good thing. So when things change roll with it. After the initial frustration with the change, you will almost always find you enjoy the change.

Take Action

You now have the knowledge you need to be successful with marketing your child care business online. Don't let the time, money, and effort you invested to get this knowledge go to waste.

Use the action plan as a map, and start moving forward.

Remember:

Success favors those in motion.

ACTION PLAN

Use this action plan as a road map. But like any trip from coast to coast there are many ways to get to the destination.

If you are already doing very well in an online marketing area, skim over the action steps. To ensure the greatest results you should check to make sure everything is in order but might not need to spend much time in that area.

You could have come across something in this book and action plan that you just know will be transformational to your child care. If that is the case, then go there now and start. This action plan is not meant to keep you from experiencing success. Just make sure once you have completed your first tasks that you return to the other parts of this book and complete those too.

Just like a four legged stool will do okay with one leg gone for a while, it will eventually have trouble, and most likely at a very bad time for you. You need to make sure all the legs of your online marketing are complete.

1. **Website.** First get your website in order. This is the foundation for which the rest of your online marketing efforts will be based. No matter where people are coming from online, at some point they will hit your website. Make sure your site looks good, fits your personality, and is easy to navigate.
2. **SEO.** Make sure your on and off page SEO is done correctly. The more challenging it is for someone to find your website the more likely they are to choose your competitor. Good SEO will make your site easy to be found and enhance your professional image. SEO can also

take a bit of time to fully settle, so the sooner you get on it the better.

3. **Maps and Google Places**. Your parents and prospects are searching online for local business they want to work with. You need to be on Google Places so you can be found when and where they are looking. This is third because the better your website's foundation is the easier and quicker you will get results on Google Places.

4. **Reviews and Testimonials**. This is all about social proof. People believe what others say about you far more than what you say about yourself. They want to hear from people just like themselves what it is like to leave their kids with you.

5. **Social Media.** Social media, especially Facebook, is where your clientele is hanging out and talking about you and their child care needs. You need to be here so you can form those relationships that lead to long term clients. Realize before they enroll they will check out your website, social media sites, and reviews.

6. **Advanced marketing.** Adwords, Mobile, QR codes – You may get to this point and find your enrollments are already doing great. Congratulations! But don't skip these steps. Advanced marketing can give you that boost when you need it and ensure you are always in the lead with your marketing efforts.

Enjoy! I look forward to hearing about the success that I know you will have. Your successes always bring cheer to me and my team in the office, so when you have those great successes please let me know by dropping me a line at onlinebook@childcare-marketing.com and also visit my website at childcare-marketing.com for more tips on growing your child care business.

GLOSSARY

A

Adwords – Google's main advertising product that offers pay-per-click advertising.

Anchor Text - the visible, clickable text in a hyperlink. The words contained in the anchor text can determine the ranking that the page will receive by search engines.

B

Bit - The smallest measurement of digital information read by computers.

Bandwidth - The rate/speed information travels from one place to another either inside a computer or between computers. Bandwidth is usually measured in bits per second, kilobits (thousands of bits) per second or megabits (millions of bits) per second. For instance, a 56K modem allows for a connection of 56 kilobits per second.

Bookmark - Like a traditional bookmark, this digital version is for marking a place on the Internet that is interesting or frequently visited, so that a user can go back to the site(s) without having to remember or retype the Internet address.

Boot - to start a computer or computer program.

Bots – See Spider

Browser - A software product that lets you find, see, and hear material on the World Wide Web, including text, graphics, sound, and video. There are many different kinds of Web browsers, the most popular being Netscape Navigator and Microsoft Internet Explorer.

Byte - Bytes are a basic measurement of computer memory. A byte is made up of eight bits.

C

Cache - A cache is the location on a computer's hard drive where the Web browser stores information (text, graphics, sounds, etc.) from Web pages or other Internet sites that have been visited recently so that returning to those pages or sites is faster and easier.

CD-ROM - "Compact Disk Read Only Memory"- a computer disk that can store large amounts of information. Special CD-ROM drives on computers playback the information although cannot save any new data.

Chat - A feature of Internet online services or Web sites that allows participants to communicate in "real time" by typing messages back and forth. After a user types a message on his/her computer, and sends it, it is instantly displayed on the computer screen(s) of another user or users.

Cookie - A piece of personal information that an Internet Web browser saves and sends back to a Web server when the user revisits a Web site. The server recognizes the information from the browser, thus identifying the user. Cookies can contain information such as user preferences, log-in or registration information, e-commerce online shopping patterns, or history of recently visited Web sites. Most Web browsers will allow users to "disable" the cookie feature, if that's preferred.

Cyberspace - is the vast area shared by the connected computers and servers of the Internet. The prefix "cyber-" is synonymous with anything having to do with the Internet.

D

Directories - similar to search engines, this is a software application that distinguishes Internet Web sites by categories for easy search by users. Users enter "keywords" to direct the application to list Web sites containing the desired information.

Domain name - An Internet Web site address reserved by a user, usually followed by .com, .net, .org or .edu.

Download - Copying or transmitting data or other information from a remote computer or server to be stored on the hard drive of a user's computer.

DSL - Digital Subscriber Line - A new technology that allows high-speed access of the Internet over standard phone lines.

E

Electronic Mail (E-Mail) - A way of sending messages and information electronically from one computer to another. Users can electronically send letters, and other text-based messages, as well as multimedia documents. New "information appliances" (including hand held devices) other than computers are also capable of sending e-mail.

Emoticons - combinations of type written characters that help a user express emotion or action when composing e-mail, an Instant Message or chatting. One example would be the smiley face :-)

F

FAQ ("Frequently Asked Questions") – help for users about a specific Web site, mailing list, product, or game. It is always a good idea for parents to find the FAQ of a certain Web site or other area of the Internet to quickly investigate or get informed about that site.

Firewall - a security program that places an electronic "wall" around a computer or network of computers, keeping it from being accessible to the general public.

File Transfer Protocol (FTP) - a software application that allows users to transfer ("download" or "upload") files from one computer to another.

G

GIF - popular format for files used to display pictures or graphics on a Web site or other section of the Internet.

H

Hacker - A person who tries to break into a computer system.

Hardware - The tangible parts of a computer and its peripherals (printer, modem, etc.)

Home Page - The first page of a Web site. This page usually contains most of the links to the content areas of the site.

Hyperlink ("link") - Instant transfer from one Internet Web page to another. A hyperlink may be text based or in the form of an image or portion of an image. The user may be linked to another page within the same Web site or to another site altogether. A user may configure his/her Web browser to identify hyperlinks by change of color (blue for instance) or change of font style (underlined or in italics). When a user's computer mouse cursor "hovers" over the hyperlink, the cursor changes shape to indicate the transfer option. By clicking the computer mouse, the user is transferred to the linked Web page.

HTML - Hypertext Markup Language - The standard language used for creating Web pages and other documents on the World Wide Web.

HTTP - Hypertext Transfer Protocol - The standard language used by computers connected to the Internet to communicate with each other.

I

Icon - a small picture that represents either text based information or a "link" to another Web page.

IFO – Irresistible Free Offer – relating to list building. Used to grab someone's attention.

Information Superhighway - refers to the Internet, the large and vast group of computers all connected via a series of workstations, networks, servers and personal computers.

Instant Message (IM) – computer software that allows users to communicate simultaneously with each other one-on-one in "real time."

Internet - A collection of thousands of computers and computer networks connected to each other.

Internet Service Provider (ISP) - A company that provides access to the Internet, most often through a local phone number. ISP's can be small companies with only a handful of subscribers or large companies with millions of subscribers.

Internet Protocol (IP) - The computer language that allows software programs to communicate with each other over the Internet.

Intranet - A private network that works like the Internet, except that it can only be accessed by a select group of people, such as the employees of a company.

J

Java - A computer programming language that allows Internet Web pages to contain animation and other special effects. Java also allows users to view the different effects in a consistent way regardless of what kind of Internet Web browser is being used.

Java Script

JPEG - a popular format for files used to display images on a Web page or other section of the Internet. These files are more compact than "GIF" files.

K

Keyword(s) – The word(s) used when using search engines or directories to find information on the Web. A user types the keyword(s) into a search "window," to allow criteria for the search. The search engine or directory will then list Web pages containing those words.

Keyword Density – The percentage of times your keyword in shown on a page relative to the total number of words. If you keywords is 5 out of 100 words you would have a keyword density of 5%.

Keyword Stuffing – The act of placing your keywords online at an unnatural rate or in locations where they are not approved.

L

Link (or "hyperlink") - Instant transfer from one Internet Web page to another. A hyperlink may be text based or in the form of an image or portion of an image. The user may be linked to another page within the same Web site or to another site altogether. A user may configure his/her Web browser to identify hyperlinks by change of color (blue for instance) or change of font style (underlined or in italics). When a user's computer mouse cursor "hovers" over the hyperlink, the cursor changes shape to indicate the transfer option. By clicking the computer mouse, the user is transferred to the linked Web page.

Log-off - to disconnect from the Internet or other on-line connection or to shutdown a computer.

M

Mailing List - similar to listserv, this is an e-mailing list users can subscribe to. Most mailing lists focus on a certain subject or common trait among its members (parents, for example).

Modem - A hardware device installed inside a computer that allows it to communicate with other computers over telephone lines. A modem enables "dial-up" access to the Internet. Modems are defined by the speed in which data may travel through it.

Mouse - A hand-held peripheral hardware device attached to your computer, which allows users to give commands to the computer by clicking a button on the device.

Multimedia - A combination of two or more types of information such as text, images, graphics, audio, and video.

N

Newsgroups - are discussion groups on the Internet focusing on a specific topic or topics where users can read and "post" comments (similar to a traditional bulletin board). Newsgroups, which have no connection to news organizations or current events, cover a wide variety of topics.

Glossary

O

P

Parental controls - software and/or online features that enable parents to monitor, track and filter the content to which their children have access.

Password - a secret word or other alphanumeric combination to control user access to a computer program, Web site or other area of the Internet. Parents may find using passwords vital in their efforts to monitor access their children have to online content.

PPC – Pay per click – an advertising system where you only pay for traffic when visitor click on your ad.

Plug-in - a software program that works with Internet Web browsers to play audio and video.

Posting – The "uploading" of a message from the user's computer screen to a discussion group or other public message area on the Internet. The message itself is called a "post."

Q

QR Code – Quick response code.

R

Robot – See Spiders

S

Search directory – similar to search engines, this is a software application that groups Internet Web sites by categories for easy search by users. Users enter "keywords" to direct the application to list Web sites containing the desired information.

Search engine - a software application that allows users of the Internet to "search" or locate information available among the millions of Internet Web pages. By typing in "keywords," users can search for Web sites that contain the information desired.

Server - a large capacity computer or group of computers that stores information and/or software programs and makes them available to users through the Internet.

Software - A computer program that gives your computer operating system directions to perform a certain task or group of tasks. Computer programmers write computer code into the software programs to perform these tasks.

Spam - inappropriately unsolicited "junk" e-mail or other messages (and postings) from hackers, commercial advertisers, or adult Web site operators. Many times spam is sent to large blocks of e-mail addresses or through other online message systems.

Spider - A software program that "crawls" through the Internet, searching through millions of Internet Web pages and Web sites and indexing information in a database. Most search engines and search directories would use a "spider" to help users track down information on the Internet.

T

Transmission Control Protocol / Internet Protocol (TCP/IP) - A computer "language" that allows for transmission of information across the Internet.

U

Upload - Copying or transmitting data and other information from your computer to another computer or server.

Uniform Resource Locator (URL) - The Internet's designated address of a Web site. Each Internet Web site is assigned a URL in order for a user to access the site. The URL may contain a domain name or other alphanumeric combinations.

V

Virus - programming code that can be attached to computer files that will damage or destroy other vital computer files and information. Many viruses are transferred during downloads of application files from the Internet that may be "infected" with the virus code.

W

Web (World Wide Web) - a part of the Internet that features information delivered publicly through text and graphical design. Web servers host the different Web pages and Web sites, which may feature not only text, but pictures, graphics, animation and sound. Users must have a Web browser to access the graphical information.

Web-based e-mail and Instant Messaging - e-mail and Instant Messaging services offered by a Web site and not directly from the Internet Service Provider, or independent software. This type of e-mail and Instant Messaging can be accessed from any computer using a Web browser.

Webmaster - the designer and administrator responsible for the creation, management and updates of an Internet Web site.

X

Y

Z

HAVE THE AUTHOR SPEAK TO YOUR GROUP, ASSOCIATION OR COMPANY

Devin Murray

Devin Murray is the leading expert in online marketing for child care and early education program. His speeches and training help owners, directors, teachers and staff to effectively marketing online to increase enrollments and family retention. Focusing exclusively on child care Devin understand the unique issues, challenges and rewards. Devin is the author of several books including *Child Care Marketing Online* and *Business Lessons from the Cockpit*.

Devin Murray is available for:

- Conferences (nationwide, regional, state or local)
- Meetings
- Corporate or Association Training
- Web Training and Events
- Leadership gathering
- Seminars
- Keynote Speaker
- Marketing and Sales Retreats

Topics (A brief overview of points covered)

9) **Social Media for Child Care Professionals-** How to utilize social media including Facebook, Pinterest, Twitter and LinkedIn to grow leads, and engage parents.

10) **List Building** - Having a large responsive list is one of the surest ways to guarantee your program is always full. Learn why, and how to grow your list.

11) **Google Places and Maps** - Parents today start their search on the internet. Often this means Google Local Business Listings, Why and how to make sure you are showing up where your prospects are looking for you.

12) **How to Get Testimonials and Review** -This presentation teaches you how to get testimonial and reviews for parents that work. You will learn how and why video testimonials are changing the landscape. You will also learn how to use the testimonials you have on more places than just your website to grow your social proof and enrollments.

13) **Maximize Your Marketing** – Easy systems to save you time and grow your enrollments

14) **4 Pillars of Effective Marketing for Child Care Leaders** – Learn how to create a stable and powerful marketing system that delivers long term success.

15) **How to Get Your Website to the Top of Google -** Having a website nobody finds is useless. In this talk you will learn the easy, step-by-step process to move your website to the top of the search engine

16) **Half Day, Day and Multi-Day Training -** Workshop style training to not only teach how to use technology but to ensure all attendees leave having used and set up their systems correctly.

Why Devin?

Unique selling points...

⇒ Devin is one of only a handful or professional speakers who focuses solely on the child care industry, its needs and issues

⇒ Devin is the author of several books

⇒ Devin is the COO of Child Care Marketing Solutions a company dedicated to educating and help early education professionals

⇒ Devin is a certified Google partner and Google Engage Company Owner

⇒ Devin is a certified educator and instructor with years of experience teaching individuals of all experience levels.

Perfect Audiences...

⇒ Owners who want to worry less about their centers and enjoy their life more

⇒ Directors who want to see their centers full and have more time not less

⇒ Teachers who have been tasked with helping grow enrollment but have never been taught marketing

⇒ Any child care professional who is struggling to understand what marketing is working wants to not waste money of what doesn't

⇒ Anyone who is helping child care owners and directors increase enrollments

Did you Know?

- Devin is available for multiple concurrent sessions
- Devin does online workshops so nobody needs to travel
- The same techniques Devin teaches will work to grow your association membership—he can show you how

To check availability contact:

Toll Free : 877-254-4619

Devin@ChildCare-Marketing.com

www.ChildCare-Marketing.com

EDUCATIONAL RESOURCES

Looking for more ways to grow your enrollment, make more money and live an easier life? Child Care Marketing has a complete catalog of educational and training material to help you succeed.

Learn more at: www.Childcare-Marketing.com

Study with the Author

Looking For More?

Check out the Study with the Author series. Listen as Devin talks you through each chapter and adds additional details answering questions from child care leaders just like you.

- Audio training to accompany each chapter
- Special webinars and audios covering chapter topics pulled from the vault and not available anywhere else
- Tools links and resources to help you achieve more faster
- Much more

Learn more at:
www.ChildCareMarketingOnline.com

27198181R00082

Made in the USA
Lexington, KY
31 October 2013